Parking Precious
& Other Off Road Tales

A
Sherri's Turn
Collection

SHERRI KUKLA

Join the Reader List!

Get an email whenever we release a new book or digital magazine and be one of the first to read the latest release! Send your name and email address to Sherri Kukla at ssormag@gmail.com

www.ssorm.com

PARKING PRECIOUS
© 2021 S&S Publishing Inc.
Published by S&S Publishing
www.ssorm.com

ISBN: 978-1-7349484-6-2

You will seek Me and find Me
when you search for Me
with all your heart.
Jeremiah 29:13

Cover Photo: It's a fun photo that has absolutely nothing to do with any of the stories in this book except it's an off road shot that includes our granddaughter Summer out on this truck's maiden voyage with the guy-in-the-garage and his good friend Jack Reilly, owner of the truck that provided them hours of adventure that day including a blow out and running out of gas.

Dedicated to the readers of S&S Off Road Magazine who have expressed much love for the Sherri's Turn columns

Your words of encouragement over the years mean more than I can ever say. And that's saying a lot, because I usually have plenty to say!

Chapter 1

Published December 1992

It was about this time of year Precious got it's name.

It was a few years back. Before kids. Before there was never enough time. Before the guy-in-the-garage spent more time working on bikes for kids and neighbors than on his own stuff.

He loved working in the garage. Building things. Fabricating they call it. Working with metal.

He used to have me help him. I learned a new word even. Template. I'd never heard of the word until I made one. It was for a grill guard on an old GMC 4x4 he had. It was a huge grill guard.

That's the first thing I remember watching him make. Other things came along. Roll cages for Baja Bugs, massive pipe bumpers for trucks, motorcycle stops for the inside of vans, front beams, piggy banks, exhaust pipes, dune buggy bumpers, a chassis or two. The guy-in-the-garage loved welding metal together. And he created some pretty useful stuff too.

But the thing that stands out most in my mind is Precious.

A flatbed trailer it was. So impressively done that even the folks at DMV commented on the clean welds and master workmanship that had gone into the project, when he went down to get it registered and licensed.

Every inch of it was painted battleship gray, right down to the plywood flooring. It was heavy duty. Carried a lot of bikes and firewood. Made a lot of trips to the desert.

He kept it parked to the side of the driveway.

One Christmas Eve I came home from shopping and parked our '62 Chevy pickup in the driveway next to the trailer. Okay, maybe I was a tad too close to it.

A little history on the '62 pickup. It was another project. You know how these guy-in-the-garages are. Everything is a project.

We had picked up the Chevy for about a thousand bucks a few years back and he was slowly restoring it, while I drove it as my daily transportation. It had been carpeted and upholstered. Dents had been removed. And it had recently been painted. Metallic gun metal gray or maybe a hair darker. Some might even have called it black.

Early that evening we loaded Christmas gifts into the truck and were planning on spending a fun-filled Christmas Eve eating dinner and opening presents at his parents' home.

But that was before he tried to back the Chevy out of the driveway.

As we were backing out, he was saying something about how I was a little close to the trailer. That's when it happened. The fender of the newly painted '62 Chevy project caught on the fender of the newly painted trailer project and the sound it made just wasn't a good sound to hear on Christmas Eve. Sort of a screeching, scraping noise that might lead you to believe metal was being twisted into grotesque shapes.

He took the truck out of reverse and eased it forward slightly. I imagined that would work kind of like putting the whole bad scene on rewind, so that presto, it would all be fixed. Not. In fact we heard the same horrid screeching noises just in a slightly different pitch.

I wasn't about to look at the guy-in-the-garage. But even without seeing the look on his face I could tell by the eloquent words leaving his mouth that he really wasn't all that happy with me or this situation that my parking job had gotten us into. He got out of the truck to look things over and found that the truck and trailer were now stuck together as if they were one big happy project.

It took some pulling and pushing, kicking and grunting, bending and yelling and finally the two vehicles were detached from each other. But equally detached, at least from an emotional standpoint, were the two occupants of the truck, namely myself and the guy-in-the-garage.

He went ahead and backed the truck out and headed to his mother's house for our jolly Christmas celebration but when we arrived, I refused to go in. In fact, I got out of the truck, walked to the back, climbed into the camper and there I sat. "I'm not going in," I said. "Your trailer is more important to you than I am."

He thought about that for a while, probably longer than was necessary and finally assured me that wasn't true. He really was between a rock and a hard spot at that moment because there was no way he could go face his mom with me pouting in the truck. She'd know in a heartbeat it was all his fault and she'd tell him so. Finally he apologized enough to get me out of the truck and sort of in a mood to celebrate Christmas, but soon after that the trailer was dubbed Precious and after a decade or so the name is still around.

Since then, Precious has been replaced by Precious II, a fully-enclosed 20-footer that makes life easier when it comes to hauling seven kids, six bikes, 60 gallons of gas and a ton of firewood. But the fun only just begins when we get home and it's time to park Precious.

I'm happy to say I've never parked a vehicle so close to Precious II that it's gotten hit. But there was that one time when I was giving hand signals to guide the guy-in-the-garage as he was parking and the house just jumped out and hit the trailer. Oops.

There comes a time in a man's life when he's just got to decide what's more important: the wife or the trailer? And having made the decision, he probably better keep the answer a secret.

Chapter 2

Published September 1996

shuddered when I saw the sight. It brought back memories of the most horrible kinds.

I was driving down the street minding my own business when out of the corner of my eye I caught a glimpse of a guy standing on the sidewalk. Uninformed individuals would think he was just a loiterer. People who aren't in the know would think he was just hanging out with nothing better to do on a summer afternoon. But I – who had often been in that same position – knew what horrible things were about to happen.

Because I recognized the awkward stance of the lone individual on the sidewalk, I knew to look for the additional signs of impending disaster. And sure enough, I turned my head a little farther to look out the window as I passed, and I saw it.

The motorhome. And worse. The trailer attached to the motorhome.

Are you catching on now? Do you know what terrible doom awaits the lone individual on the sidewalk?

Yes, it's true. His summer day was just about to be ruined as he accepted the thankless task of directing the driver of the motorhome.

Maybe you think I exaggerate. Well, then you haven't been there.

What about the time the trailer hit the house?

Hey, I thought the guy-in-the-garage knew what he was doing. Okay, sure, he told me to watch and tell him where to go while he was backing the enclosed trailer onto the side of the house. Well, I can't see everything. Besides, how was I supposed to know he was going to hit the house until he hit it?

You're not buying these lame excuses? Don't feel left out. Neither did he. At least it didn't leave any damage, just a few little scrape marks on the eaves.

Now, the city bus. That was a different story.

It was dark out. He was backing the motorhome out from its hideaway on the other side of the house. I'm supposed to stand across the street and motion for him when it's clear.

Well, first of all, in my defense: It's dark and I can't see his face in the side mirror so I don't know for sure exactly if he can see me. I stand in various places on the sidewalk, staring, glaring and squinting across the street to see if I can see his face in the mirror so I know he can see me. He slowly starts backing down the lawn and as he gets to the sidewalk, he stops. That's where my job starts. I'm supposed to watch for cars on this busy street we live on and then motion him when it's all clear.

There's just one problem. It always is clear until just after I motion him. Then he starts going and the cars start coming. Only this time it was a city bus. A big, maroon, Chula Vista Transit bus. And I saw it coming just as he was pulling off the sidewalk. I knew he couldn't see it yet. I also knew he couldn't see me anymore. So I just stood there, eyes bugging out, fists clinched, teeth grinding, hoping that things would turn out okay.

Well, I'm sure he was just a little startled when he got onto the street only to be facing headlight to headlight with a big city bus.

At least the motorhome was nearly the same size and he was able to look straight in the eye of the bus driver. He let me know how he felt about that encounter as soon as he got the motorhome safely parked.

We've since modified our plans for me directing him out onto the street.

Or how about having to guide him as he backs the motorhome up to hitch the trailer. We're talking an eight-foot wide motorhome that you want me to direct up over the curb into the driveway onto a two-inch wide tow ball. He claims he can't read my hand signals and I wonder why getting him within two to three inches of his destination is not good enough.

At least once we get to the desert I don't have to worry about causing problems with the motorhome. Of course there was that one time when I left the key on for four days and we didn't discover it until the last day. The wind was blowing something fierce, had been for several days. We piled in, tired and a little cranky, more than ready to leave, but the motorhome wouldn't start . . . well, that's another story.

Chapter 3

Published April 1999

I distinctly remember the guy-in-the-garage telling me that this time the vehicle we were about to purchase was definitely race-ready. No tear down needed. Just buy it. Bring it home. Race it.

So was it just my imagination a few weeks later when I saw him cutting the top off the cage of the Chenowth Magnum he had assured me was "race-ready"? Admittedly, he had no choice. A rule change after he acquired the vehicle, forced him to change the height of the car.

But this wasn't the first time he'd cut a frame in two.

In the early seventies, it seemed like it was all the rage to lower the frame on motorcycles, especially ones of the flat track variety. You could even buy lowering kits that came with the little pieces you'd have to weld in once you cut the frame in two.

Imagine the thrill in his father's voice, when he stepped out into the garage and saw the teenage version of the guy-in-the-garage sawing his motorcycle frame in half. The motorcycle the dad had just co-signed a loan for.

"What do you think you're doing?" Dad says in a voice that caused neighbors the next block over to wonder what he thought he was doing. "It'll never run again," Dad says, shaking his head.

But it did run.

Not every vehicle he's torn down has been for racing. The little black dune buggy, our first ever, he picked up for several hundred dollars a couple decades ago. We had a lot of fun in it the first time out. Then it was tear-down time. In retrospect I have to wonder if the fun of having an off road vehicle for these love-tools-own-a-million-welders-gotta-get-my-lathe-working type of guys isn't just tearing them down, making them better, putting them back together, selling them, buying another and starting all over.

He had so much fun working on the little buggy that he decided to sell it and just build another one from scratch.

I remember when we got down to the nitty-gritty nuts and bolts to finish it off, we went to a racing hardware store. He told me in advance what we were going to get. Didn't sound like much to me. We didn't have too much cash on hand, maybe a buck or two and I was planning on writing a check. (Why do you think he takes me along on the shopping sprees? He can cut a frame in half and weld it back together, but writing a check at the shop is a bit much.)

So while we're waiting for our turn at the counter, I notice a sign that says "No checks accepted for purchases less than $10.) I panic. I don't have enough cash. I'm supposed to be handling the finances here. He told me we were getting a couple pieces of tubing and maybe a few nuts and bolts. I figure at a couple bucks apiece, we're probably not going to make their minimum. So I say, "Do you think we're going to spend more than $10?"

He looks like he's going to laugh out loud, then manages to contain it in a brief smile and says, "Yeah, don't worry about it."

We walked out of the store later with a tiny little sack and a check register that had just logged in a hundred dollar check written at this place. A hundred bucks! And it fit in a lunch sack.

Of course, the Funco single-seater race car needed some work. That goes without saying. It was a little old.

The Baja Bug, well, of course, it had to be torn down. Originally it was just a street bug.

I'm sure there were more torn down, cut-in-two, stripped to bare metal type projects over the years, I probably just can't remember them all.

But how dumb does the guy-in-the-garage think I am?

A few years ago he got all caught up in the rekindled flat track craze, so he went out and bought himself a flat tracker. (No, he didn't write the check. I wrote it for him before he left.)

Came home and told me. "This bike is all ready to race. I won't have to do anything to it."

Well, if that's true, why is it a few months later when I looked in the garage, the seat was different, the gas tank was different, the fender was different, the exhaust pipe was different, the brakes were different, the shocks were different, the handlebars were different?

Race-ready indeed. I'll never fall for that line again.

Chapter 4

Published August 2001

I had been gone most of the day and the guy-in-the-garage was home with all the kids. I pulled into the driveway after dark and was greeted by some hungry folks who knew I had a car full of groceries.

I went into the house and looked around for the guy-in-the-garage. He was nowhere to be found. At least not inside the house.

I made my way to the garage, which I might add, is not near the driveway I had parked in. It's at the other end of the house, so we'll give him credit and assume he didn't hear me pull up.

I opened the garage door and there he sat surrounded by tools, projects and country music. He looked up and smiled.

"You know," I said to him, "the kids have asked me if you love me as much as I love you?"

He cocked his head sideways, kind of like a dog who doesn't understand what you're saying. "Huh?" he said and then snuck a look back down at the intricate project he was holding with his hands and balancing on his lap.

"Well, you know how I always wait up for you and watch for you at the door when you're coming home?" I asked.

He smiled and said "Yeah," then snuck another look down at the project that was taking up both hands. This time he even made a little adjustment to the items before looking back up at me, still smiling.

I began to wonder: What makes him smile? My return home or the gadget in his hands?

"Well, the youngest one asked me why you don't wait up or watch for me at the door like I do for you. She said she thinks it's because I love you more than you love me."

"Really?" he said struggling to maintain eye contact.

"Really," I said.

We stared into each other's eyes for a moment and then he broke the silence with those special words I have heard so many times over the years: "Can you help me with this?" He held up the contraption he was working with.

While I was helping him I scanned the garage and began counting motorcycles. I'm sure there were not this many here this time last week. As a matter of fact, he is buying new projects faster than people can submit classifieds. It's gotten so bad that the classifieds actually come in now with special little notes attached "for Steve in case he is interested."

When I finished helping him with that item we moved across the garage to another task that needed an extra hand. "Hold this right here," he said while he picked up a hammer.

"You're not going to miss and hit my hand are you?" I said.

"I hope not," was about as reassuring as he could get. The smile scared me.

It took me back to the days he was building a Chenowth two-seat buggy in the garage and he had me holding the seats down while he was drilling brackets underneath.

"You're not going to accidently drill right up through the seat and into my hand, are you?" I remember that awful fear as I pressed down on the seats, and could feel the drill just inches away.

"I hope not," he said.

And then there was the time he had me holding pieces to an exhaust system while he tack-welded them. I could feel sparks flying all over and I just knew they were going to land on me.

"You're not going to burn me, are you?" I asked.

"Hope not," he said and kept welding.

I came out to the garage a little later in the evening to announce that dinner was ready.

"Be right in," he said intently working on some important aspect of his current project. He barely looked up.

"You're not going to take forever and let dinner get cold, are you?" I asked.

He looked up and smiled. "Hope not," he said.

But we both knew that even though he intended to come right in he'd likely get carried away trying to finish up one little thing. And though I fully intended to get mad at him for not coming in while dinner was hot, I'd likely overlook it, once again.

Because there is something worse in life than eating cold mashed potatoes and chicken for dinner. And that is living with a guy-in-the-garage when he has nothing to do in the garage.

Chapter 5

Published August 2002

Some time ago I mentioned in this column about the freezer in my office.

It provided a nice background humming noise whenever the motor kicked in for whatever reason freezers do that sort of thing.

I know I'm luckier than most. A lot of people don't have freezers in their office.

It all started because that office was just a little too close to the garage. One day as the guy-in-the-garage was trying to figure out where to put his latest motorcycle purchase, it occurred to him that he would have a lot more room if he got the freezer out of the garage.

He first checked out the kitchen and I think was just about ready to stick it in there, when I reminded him that the kitchen was not large enough for a refrigerator and an upright freezer and everything else that belongs in a kitchen.

Well, he was not to be discouraged. This was a man on a mission. And it didn't take him long to figure out where to put the albatross. He started suspiciously eyeing that little office of mine. The one that was way too close to the garage.

I could tell by the look on his face he was going to move it a few feet through the doorway and plop it right in my office.

"Where are you going to put it?" I said, motioning to show him there wasn't an available square inch of space.

He stared at a large white cabinet sitting against the wall. "It could go right here."

I wondered if he was blind.

"There is a cabinet there," I said.

"You don't really use that, do you?"

A few of the projects that helped displace me and my office.

Now, there's a funny thing about that choice of words. Whenever he starts a sentence or question off with, "You don't" and ends with "do you?" it usually means he is going to get something he wants by talking me out of something I have, need, want, desire or am doing.

This was no exception. I took a look inside the cabinet and had to acknowledge that if I was slightly more organized as well as in the mood to de-clutter my life, I could probably fit everything in

19

that cabinet into another small storage area.

It comes as no surprise to you that the freezer did get moved from the garage to the office.

But there *is* a surprise ending to this story.

That is, that the freezer is no longer in that office. It has been moved back out into the garage.

After all of that, you might be wondering if the guy-in-the-garage had a run-in with conscience, or even more unimaginable, decided to part with some motorcycles.

No the truth is, not only is the freezer gone from that office, but so am I.

That nice little office right off the garage became his brand new "engine room." And there is no room in an "engine room" for a freezer.

Not only did the freezer leave once he took possession of my space, but new shelves went in, pictures popped up all over the walls, new lighting, new paint, new screen door for the slider so he has a nice breeze when he works. I never felt that nice breeze. As long as it was my office, he kept saying that someday he was going to replace the screen so we could have a nice breeze.

Well "someday" finally came.

Of course I'm probably being a little unfair here. Because once he decided to boot me out of that office, he pointed out a better room for my office. And I have to admit that to encourage me to leave that space he wanted with as little complaining as possible, he painted the new office, put in lighting, new window coverings, electrical outlets installed right where I wanted them and even hung pictures for me.

But, as I write this column, and look around to admire my new office, I'm noticing that some other things have found their way into these new quarters of mine.

A wheel and tire off a motorcycle, a set of front forks, a box that looks like it probably has brand new motorcycle handlebars in it. And over in the corner there is some motorcycle memorabilia.

I guess I better enjoy this space while it's still mine. I have a feeling one of these days he's going to walk in here and say, "You don't really need all this space, do you?"

Chapter 6

Published May 2005

How hard could it be to sell a hot dog?

That's what I thought a few years back when a friend asked me if I wanted to work in the snack bar with her at an upcoming race.

My biggest problem, I thought, was wondering if I would even be at the race. So I hemmed and hawed and after a week or two it looked like we were going to the race for sure and I said I'd be glad to help.

Did I say "glad"?

That was before I knew I was not gifted in the area of selling hot dogs. That was before I gained a new appreciation for people who work behind the counters of fast food restaurants, snack bars and ice cream parlors.

The snack bar was not an actual building. More of a big box. Wooden, not cardboard. It had holes in it. A really big hole with a counter to serve people. A hole on the side so wind could come gushing in and blow things over. And a hole in the back for a door so unsuspecting volunteers like myself could step inside and make a fool of themselves for four hours.

Well make that three hours and 20 minutes. Because every time someone I knew was racing, I went running out the back door, across the roadway and up to the fence to watch the race.

It would go something like this. Carol was cooking and putting together the Aunt Janey's Super Special Flat Track BBQ chicken sandwiches with garden fresh tomatoes (or whatever it was her husband Wayne had named them) and the hot dogs. Periodically she'd call out and tell me how many dogs she had done and ask me if I needed more.

I was supposed to keep her informed of pending orders; refill the tubs of ice with drinks when they ran low and hand out candy and food as people ordered it.

That would have worked fine if the people would have cooperated. But what they did was all gather in a group somewhere off to the side where we couldn't see them and then about 20 people would line up all at once at the window.

"What can I get for you?" I'd say.

"A Diet Coke, two hot dogs--what do you want, son?--an ice tea? Do you have ice tea? Make that two ice teas, never mind the Diet Coke, and let's have three hot dogs instead of two and what kind of candy did you want son?--they have--what kind of candy do you have?--oh, look over here, son--here's all the wrappers on the menu board--see what they have--what do you want son?"

Son would say "Mmm, umm, I'm thinking . . . ."

"Hurry up son, people are waiting, what kind of candy do you want--how about the chocolate? Do you want the chocolate? No, how about the Starbursts? Mmm-mmm Starbursts are good, do you want Starbursts?" Then back to me. "Okay we'll have Starbursts with everything else."

Everything else? I got so busy wondering what kind of candy the kid was going to pick and how long it would take him to pick it that I forgot about the rest of the order.

"What did you say you wanted?"

"Ice tea, two cans, three hot dogs."

"Three hot dogs, Carol!" Oops. Forgot to replenish the tea in the ice tub. "I'm sorry, the tea isn't cold, do you want something else?"

Well it got worse as the night went on. We ran out of chocolate candy; and we ran out of Starbursts and we ran out of hot dogs and hot dog buns.

Not only was I not very good in the food department, but I failed miserably in the information department too.

Along with trying to keep orders straight, keep the cooler replenished, and keep track of what we were out of so I could mark it off the menu, I got asked all kinds of questions. How long has this track been here? Is there development slated for this area? How much longer do you think this track will be here? What kind of bikes are out on the track now? How many heats are there tonight? How much does it cost to race here? How long has this group been together that's putting on the races? When is the next race? Where can I get a copy of a race schedule? What other places around here do they do these kinds of races? What year are the bikes that are out there running right now?

I had one pat answer: "I don't know. Do you want a hot dog?"

To comfort myself I silently practiced answering the question that I knew would come at the end of the evening. "No, Carol, I don't want to work in the snack bar again." I repeated it silently over and over.

Fortunately everyone was incredibly patient. We didn't hear one complaint. Unless you count the guy who came up, looked us over, looked the snack bar over and smirked "So this is the snack bar?!" and walked away.

And then came the inevitable question. "Do you want to work in the snack bar again at the next race?" Carol asked as we cleaned up.

I looked her straight in the eye and said, "Okay."

Chapter 7

Published December 2007

I first met her when I was 16 years old. She was pretty thrilled to finally have another female in the family, not that I was actually in the family yet. But believe me I was working on that.

One of her favorite memories of my early days that I heard her tell a number of times over the years, was about the afternoon I sat in The King's chair. What I mean by "The King" of course is the head of the household. The recliner that no one sat in but him. The man that no one spoke back to, no one questioned.

I have no recollection of the incident but she tells that I was relaxing in this chair when he entered the room and said "You're sitting in my chair."

She said I looked at him and casually commented "I don't see your name on it."

And everyone else in the house held their breath to see what would happen next. They were all stunned when he sauntered over to the couch and sat down, leaving me to enjoy The Chair.

I think that must have been the day I really secured a special place deep in her heart.

You always knew where you stood on just about any topic with her, she loved a good debate (polite word for argument).

But despite that penchant for arguing and debating we never doubted her love. And though it seems uncommon for a mother-in-law to be devoted to a daughter-in-law, I would have to say that would be a good way to describe our relationship.

I remember her telling me once many years ago that if the guy-in-the-garage and I ever had a disagreement that led to one of us moving back home, I was welcome to come to her house but he was not.

She loved buying things for us. Someone close once said to me "My mother-in-law buys me a set of wooden spoons. Your mother-in-law buys you a washing machine."

1970. This is where it all began. We never stop missing them.

She loved to take me shopping and I had to be careful what I looked at as we strolled through the stores, because she wanted to buy everything that caught my eye.

One time on a tourist shopping spree in the historical town of Julian she nearly got us killed. Of course I'm exaggerating, but I did threaten never to go out in public with her again after that day.

We were getting ready to cross a street and there was traffic lined up at the stop sign and lots of people flowing back and forth in the crosswalk, so it's likely the rough looking guy on the chopper might have grown impatient. As we crossed in front of his motorcycle he revved his engine. Later at home when I related the story to the rest of the family I said he was probably just revving it because it wasn't idling right and he didn't want it to stall. But my mother-in-law told that he GUNNED his motor loudly at us in a threatening manner to let us know he was ready to run us over and she let loose with some loud words to let him know how she felt about that threat. I expected him to really come after us then and I told her that day "I will never go out in public with you again!"

But of course I did and many times in the following years we discussed that story and neither one of us ever changed our versions to agree with the other.

"My son did that, didn't he!" she said vehemently one day after picking me up from my mother's house for a lunch outing. While sitting in her car she was looking at a gaping hole in the outer wall of the house. I admitted to her that yes, it was her son who had put the hole in the house while testing his new dune buggy in the front yard. She shook her head in disgust and then uttered the line she was famous for whenever she got really frustrated with one or both of her sons: "I should have had parakeets!"

Memories of her wouldn't be complete without reflecting on the mounds and mounds of M&M cookies she baked over the years. Every fall and winter was cookie-baking time for many many years and when she baked, it wasn't just a dozen or two. It was piles and piles and piles of cookies. They were all over the table in huge Tupperware containers, all over the kitchen counters, it was like they took over the kitchen and dining room. And these were huge cookies. Unforgettable cookies. In fact whenever we run across childhood friends of the guy-in-the-garage it's not uncommon for them to remember the cookies and the brownies they ate in her kitchen after school.

"I'm going to die one of these days," she was known to say now and then. "We all die one day," she would say, as if sharing some info with us we might not have known. While we didn't understand it at the time it's possible that in her own way she was comforting us before she left because she wouldn't be here after she left to do that. It was her way of preparing her family. It was her way of saying we all become a part of history sooner or later. So don't be too surprised or sad when it happens.

She was a third generation breast cancer victim, following in the path of her mother and grandmother before her, although she outlived each of them by over 20 and 40 years respectively. She survived 20 years after the initial bout.

And the fact is that no matter that she warned us that the day would come, it was still a shock when it arrived. We thought she would be around for 10 more years letting us know that she was going to be gone one day.

But this avid reader has now herself entered the history books. Not the ones in schools or on the library shelves, but the one we carry most closely to us, the history book in our hearts.

Chapter 8

Published August 2008

Since this is our volunteer special issue this month, I thought I would take some time to volunteer some information.

Oh, sure, I know that's not what the whole volunteer theme is about, but it just seems a good time to make a confession.

And the information I want to volunteer is that I am an eavesdropper and just a little bit nosy.

I admit it. I also admit that I know that the guy-in-the-garage does not appreciate that fact.

I have discovered something just recently as we are coping with the 110+ temps in Ocotillo Wells where we live. And it's bad news for eavesdroppers.

To save some money on utility bills we recently installed a swamp cooler and turned off the air conditioner. For those not familiar, the swamp cooler works like a super duty fan and it can be kind of loud when it's on. We keep a window open just a little bit in each room so the cool air will draft through and we also keep a fan going in my office. Now keep in mind that we work, live and play in Ocotillo Wells. So our house is multipurpose. The swamp cooler is in the kitchen, which is not too far from my office. To the eavesdroppers in the crowd, all these logistics are of critical importance.

If I'm sitting in my office working and the guy-in-the-garage is in the kitchen making a phone call, in the past, as in pre-swamp cooler days, all I had to do was turn down the music in my office (which is done by quickly hitting the mute button on the computer), and I could hear nearly everything he was saying. Admittedly I'm hearing a one-sided conversation, but it's enough to give me some info on what's going on with the guy.

But nowadays, I can't hear anything. I would have to go and stand right next to him while he is on the phone to be able to hear. I don't think he would appreciate that.

As a matter of fact, a couple of days ago I was actually in the kitchen early in the day putting a meat loaf in the crock pot. A call came for him and I was able to track him down on the property, which is no small feat, so he could come in and take the call. Immediately the motorcycle talk started and just as immediately my ears were tuned in to everything he was saying. This was the perfect opportunity, because I had a legitimate reason to be in the kitchen.

However, that evening I made the colossal mistake of asking him about something I had heard him saying to his friend on the phone.

Wow, he did not look happy about that.

"What were you doing? Eavesdropping again?!" he said in a not so friendly tone.

"I was right in the kitchen making YOUR dinner," I said rather indignantly, "and I just happened to hear what you were talking about."

"Oh," he grunted. "I didn't see you there."

Wow, I thought. I need to make some changes if I'm that unnoticeable.

I do have to admit though he has some legitimate reasons for being annoyed about my insatiable appetite for listening to other people's conversations.

A number of times over the years as we have been in hospital emergency rooms (not an uncommon experience for off road enthusiasts), I think I have really annoyed him by constantly reporting to him what is going on in all the cubicles around us.

Okay, so he's hooked up to machines and getting stitched on and examined and maybe he isn't that interested in the drama playing out across the hall, which I'm relating to him play by play as soon as I hear new segments. I guess when viewed that way he does have a legitimate gripe about the eavesdropping.

My best memory of overhearing a conversation was the time he bought an exhaust pipe on eBay.

Now, when I say "he bought an exhaust pipe" what I really mean is that he sat next to me and dictated every bid so that I could do all the computer work to buy this exhaust pipe, which of course is not without its hazards. Needing my help also requires that he listen to all my input and questions about what he is buying. Thinking about the 100 or so exhaust pipes he already has for vintage motorcycles, I had asked him what seemed like a simple question: "Why do you need an exhaust pipe?" He gave me what he hoped was a simple answer: "It's for my brother." The answer satisfied me and could have remained simple if not for the phone call from his brother later in the evening.

I answered the phone and while we were chatting I said "We won that exhaust pipe for you on eBay." Immediately I hear laughter and I wonder, "Why is that so funny?" Then when he can talk again, the brother-in-law-in-the-garage says, still trying to hold back chuckles, "Is that what he told you?" Suddenly it was crystal clear. We chatted a few more minutes before I hunted down the guy-in-the-garage and gave him the phone.

He walked to a far corner of the living room, actually standing near an open sliding glass door so his voice would project outside into the vast wilderness of the desert. I retreated to my office in the next room and immediately muted the music. Just in time to hear those hilarious words come out of his mouth: "Why? Did YOU tell her?"

And the big exhaust pipe secret was out of the bag. I never did get an answer for why he needed exhaust pipe number 101. For some reason neither one of us brought up the subject again.

But something else equally as devastating as the swamp cooler happened this year and it seems my days of getting endless amounts of information by being nosy have come to an end.

This formerly computer illiterate guy now has his own computer set up in a corner of my office and has learned two things that have put a halt to my information flow. He has learned how to search for items and buy them on eBay without me and worse, has learned how to send and receive email without my help.

Imagine the frustrations when I see him reading and responding to emails and I have no clue who he is talking to and what they are saying. It drives me crazy seeing him peck away at that keyboard. I could say "Who are you writing to?" and "What are you saying?" but I have a feeling that would really be annoying.

And believe me, when he leaves the office and heads to his shop I get the strongest urge to go over to his desk and read his messages both incoming and outgoing to see what I'm missing now that he has advanced to this level of communication.

But the truth is, I can't bring myself to do that. Because as much as I want to know, even a nosy eavesdropper has a certain code of ethics.

Chapter 9

Published March 2011

I thought it was bad when the guy-in-the-garage was restoring his own motorcycles, but now he's taken to restoring them for other people as well. So now instead of one project going on in his mind, he is juggling three of them.

He rarely listened to me when I talked while he was working on one project, but at least he was aware enough to know when to add a well-placed "uh-huh" as I paused to take a breath, so he could at least pretend to be listening.

Now he's got so much going on in his head it doesen't even register that I'm talking. I didn't realize how much I could miss the "uh-huh's.

Project #3 for Jack, the rare 238 Greenstreak.

But the big question of the day is "What is it about an old motorcycle that makes a grown man giddy with excitement?"

Some time ago we had big plans for a day out. That is a day without work, without all the usual hustle and bustle of our lives and a day without the motor-mouth four-year-old granddaughter who came into our lives on a permanent basis a couple years ago. We actually had a babysitter lined up and we were going to spend all day that Saturday just having fun.

That was until the 1969 Kawasaki 238 showed up for sale on the internet.

That was the day that all non-motorcycle communication ceased.

He was already working on three of his own bikes, each one of them in various stages of tear-down in addition to the Yamaha flat track project he was building for his friend Jack. But when he saw the 238 his face lit up at this rare find and he was immediately firing off emails to Jack, who had recently decided that he too needed to acquire as many vintage motorcycles as possible. Sure enough, Jack was interested and gave him the go-ahead to negotiate a deal.

It was early on a Tuesday morning and we were getting ready to head out for the day with our first destination a couple of hours away to pick up the next issue of the magazine from the printer. But before we could leave, the guy-in-the-garage was on the phone trying to start the deal for the Kawasaki. He had to leave a message. Which was the start of our problems that day.

"Did you forward the phone to the cell?" he asked.

"Yes."

"Do you have the phone with you?" he asked.

"Yes."

"Did you turn it on?" he asked.

"Yes."

It would be an understatement to say this guy was excited about this find. And unfortunately I'm the one who is in charge of the phone when we're out together, but admittedly I don't always do a great job of knowing where the phone is.

We set out from our desert home/office to the big city and I started off with the phone in my hand so I would be able to quickly answer it when the big call came. But as is often the case eventually the phone was not in my hand anymore. That is the interesting part about me trying to keep track of the phone. I don't ever exactly recall what I do with it, but somehow it goes from being right at my fingertips to me not having a clue where it is.

Riding along shotgun, I felt something funny and heard something too. It wasn't loud and it wasn't a big feeling, but I knew something had just happened and I wasn't sure what. I looked at the guy-in-the-garage and he didn't seem to notice anything. Must be nothing, I decided. Wrong thing to think.

The guy-in-the-garage was really antsy about getting the return phone call about the motorcycle. We were in and out of service areas as we drove from the desert, through the mountains, to the city, so I didn't think anything about the phone not ringing. But as we got into a full service area it suddenly occurred to me that I really didn't know where the phone was, and if it rang and I couldn't find it, we'd have a big war on our hands.

So I discreetly started looking around for the phone. The last thing I wanted was for him to know what I was doing.

But since we've been through this same scenario hundreds of times he caught on instantly.

I tried to ignore his "helpful" comments about what I should do with the phone as I kept searching.

Thankfully a fuel stop gave me the opportunity to get out of the truck and really search. That's when I discovered that the funny little sound I heard earlier was the phone slipping down in between the seat and clunking onto the floor under the seat, in a place I never could have reached while we were driving.

I triumphantly showed him the phone. He looked disgusted. I returned the look.

"You care more about getting a phone call about a rare motorcycle than about keeping me happy!"

"So I keep you happy by letting you lose the phone all the time?" he asked.

It was hard to stay mad while I was laughing at how absurd that sounded.

You're getting the picture that this return

Project #1 for Jack, the Kawasaki flat tracker. All done.

phone call was so important to him that I needed to make sure I did nothing to prevent him from taking this call.

So why wasn't I smart enough to leave the phone with him later when I had to go to the bathroom?

There we were at the printer, he was loading magazines and I headed off to the ladies room. It had been several hours since he left the message about the motorcycle and the phone hadn't rang all morning. So why is it, the very instant, the one minute in time when I definitely would not want that phone to ring, that it starts ringing? I groan and look at it, hoping desperately it's not THE call. No such luck.

Quickly I put the guy on hold, scurry out to the guy-in-the-garage and hand him the phone, then rush back to complete my business.

Later that night I learn that not only did they seal the deal but they're heading up to Bakersfield on Saturday to pick up the bike.

"Saturday?! That's when we're going out," I said.

"But that's the only day Ted can go and he really wants to go with me and Jack to get the bike," the guy-in-the-garage says pleading for mercy for the brother-in-law-in-the-garage. He tried to look sad but the ridiculous grin on his face ever since he found the motorcycle just wouldn't go away.

How do you argue against such excitement? These three have been riding together since they were kids and it made sense they would all go together to get the newest addition to their vintage collection, especially one so rare.

But the way I look at it these guys owe me big time. I gave up an outing when we already had a babysitter lined up, and took a phone call on the toilet of all places. Because the only other option was to die.

Chapter 10

Published November 2015

I was waving frantically trying to get the attention of the guy-in-the-garage and he was, to put it politely, completely ignoring me.

Completely ignoring me with a totally disgusted look on his face is another way of saying it. Completely ignoring me yet simultaneously snarling at me would even be a better way to say it.

I'm sure he was thinking that re-arranging our office would be a really great thing to do, since my desk faces his and when he sits at it to make a phone call, if I happen to look up and over the top of my computer screen I can stare right at him.

Well thankfully for him his desk does not face mine, so he actually has to turn his head to see me.

He was talking on the phone on this particular day and although he wasn't originally looking at me, I guess he could feel me staring and could sense that I wanted his attention.

He deeply regretted giving it to me.

As talented and capable as this guy is when it comes to restoring motorcycles or doing maintenance on buildings, vehicles, acreage, you name it, the one thing he absolutely cannot do is multi-task.

So if he's talking to someone on the phone and I'm trying to get his attention about something, that just shuts down his senses.

He can't understand what I want nor does he know what the person on the other end of the phone just said either. The only thing he seems capable of doing at that point is snarling, which I'm sure would have escalated to growling at me if there wasn't the risk that the person on the phone would think he was growling at them.

I'm used to all this. I know he doesn't want me to interrupt him. I know he's going to get frustrated. I know he can't listen to me and listen to someone else at the same time.

So why, one might wonder, would I interrupt him during a phone call?

Yes, he wondered that same thing. Even asked me that after he finally hung up.

"What was so important?" Do I need to say it wasn't in one of his kindest voices?

"You were giving the guy the wrong email address!" I said, and I may have sounded slightly annoyed. "I was trying to get your attention so you could give him the right one."

Did I mention how much technology annoys this guy? And though he badly wanted the motorcycle info the person on the other end of the phone could provide for him and was planning on emailing him, that did not override his desire at that moment to do away with the phone, the computer, and who knows, maybe even me!

To say he is technologically challenged would be an understatement. I have heard him threaten to shoot his computer. I have heard him threaten to throw it out the sliding glass door just inches away from his desk. And I believe he was going to do that without actually opening the door.

He complains if he gets two or three spam emails a day. I, who get hundreds every week, patiently come around my desk to his to help him try to eliminate the annoying invasions.

As much as he hates the computer, he also loves it because there he has world wide access to all things motorcycle.

Another day he was talking on the phone to a guy about restoring motorcycles, in another room I might add, so he could be undisturbed. Read that as his wife can't interfere in his conversation.

But suddenly he shows up at my side and tosses a hastily written note down on my desk, then motions frantically and whispers "get me on this website!"

> "Why would I ignore you?" he asked with just a hint of a smirk showing on his face.

I'm watching and listening to him talk to this guy on the phone as I stop everything I'm doing to open up the web browser and log onto the site he desperately needs to see. As I'm just about there I hear him say into the phone "I'm almost there, sorry our satellite is slow."

Ha! The satellite isn't the only thing slow around here.

While technology is not one of his strong points motorcycle restoration and attention to detail definitely are.

I once heard him spend nearly an hour on the phone discussing rivets. Rivets! In another room of course. He rarely talks on the phone in my presence. Seems he has learned something about the frustration of that.

Gets off the phone from rivet man, heads over to his computer with another scrawled note and says "I'm going to try to find a website."

I just about burst out laughing.

"Really?" I asked. "How are you going to do that?"

"I'm hoping you'll help me," he said and he wasn't even embarrassed.

How can it be that I'm supposed to be totally quiet and invisible until he needs my help with something. And even if he needs my help but doesn't realize it, such as in not knowing his own email address, I'm still supposed to be quiet and invisible.

I've tried. I really have, but being quiet and invisible is not one of my strong points.

I once accused him of ignoring me after he got off the phone during another incident where I had information I knew he absolutely needed.

"Why would I ignore you?" he asked with just a hint of a smirk showing on his face.

"Because you think I'm pestering you and distracting you while you're trying to do business," I said.

Now he laughed outloud. "Well, aren't you?" he said.

We have progressed a lot in the computer arena though. There was a time where he didn't have one, didn't want one, but still wanted to hang out on ebay and send emails around the world. So he would park his chair right next to my desk and dictate to me for what seemed like hours. I do not miss those days. Do. Not.

I think much faster than he does so when he would start to dictate the email, he didn't even have "Hi Bob" out of his mouth and I already typed the whole email for him because I had a vague idea of what he wanted to say anyway.

However, as helpful as I thought that was, it really just slowed the whole process down even more. Because then he would have to stop thinking so he could read what I wrote. Then he would tell me that isn't how he wanted to say it or what he wanted to say and I would sigh loudly and delete it all and patiently wait with my hands poised over the keyboard for the next word or sentence.

And why would I do that time after time? I kept hoping that the day would come when I really could speed things up for him.

Even though I know that I know that I know when he's trying to think he prefers me to be quiet and invisible.

But as hard as I try, it just ain't me.

Chapter 11

Published January 2016

Anything the guy-in-the-garage needs while I'm on deadline for the magazine is never too much to ask. In his mind.

Take today for instance. Just a few pages away from being done with the January issue, he finishes up his portion of the proofreading, then heads down to his shop.

I'm hard at work, the last day or two is always the hardest, because you reach a point where you think you'll never be finished.

My phone rings. I can tell it's a call from his shop.

"Did I leave my glass of Mountain Dew up there on my desk?" he asks.

I look around and sure enough, there it is. Ice cold. Refreshing. Mountain Dew.

"Yep, it's here," I say.

There is a pause. Then "I knew I left it up there." Then another pause. You can tell, this is a big challenge for him What to do? He's at the shop working on a customer's motorcycle and his Mountain Dew is at the house, about a three minute walk in the cold wind. He's thirsty. Needs that liquid refreshment. That pick-me-up the Dew provides.

Still the pause. So I finally say, "Do you want me to bring it down?"

He comes to life. "Hey yeah! That will be a good chance for you to take a break!"

Oh brother. This guy.

And so I took off for the three minute walk in the freezing cold windy weather carrying an ice cold drink. Of course those of you who live in snow country may not think 59 degrees is freezing, but since it's 61 degrees colder than the temps here just a few months ago, I consider it freezing.

That was today. Over the weekend my office was lively with the guy-in-the-garage corresponding with people on his computer and the 9-year-old granddaughter sitting at my side trying to solve a Nancy Drew mystery on the second computer at my desk.

I'm working away. Editing articles. Designing layouts. Identifying racers for picture captions while at the same time telling the guy-in-the-garage how to spell words for his email messages and checking to see if he is right guessing which artist is singing the Christmas songs I'm listening to on Pandora. The granddaughter is frustrated with the difficult-to-solve mystery and also needs assistance, which I try to offer all while editing and designing.

Just another day at the office.

But when time comes for the guy-in-the-garage to go back to proofreading, all the world comes to a stop.

The music gets turned off, the computers turned down, the phone calls taken in another room far from where he is and no one can talk. Essentially all of life for, say a square mile, around where he sits must be silent. Because he can't concentrate if there is noise while he's proofreading.

I often wonder if he ever sees the irony of what goes on in the office while I'm working compared to when he is working. I suppose now while he's proofreading this article it might give him a clue.

It's just that as many times as I've read time management tips that say to stop multi-tasking because you can't be productive that way, I would have to say that if I stopped multi-tasking then nothing would get done at all. At least nothing that I'm responsible for.

It's not that the guy-in-the-garage has no respect for me or my work it's more than likely because this is how we've rolled for all these years and maybe it never occurs to him it's fairly difficult for me to concentrate on so many things at once, but I just do it.

And maybe I need to understand that he just isn't wired to multi-task.

We love living in the desert, but it's a long way from just about everywhere, so when it's time to head out for errands, the list usually grows longer by the minute as we schedule the day. The guy-in-the-garage who can put in 10-12 hours a day working on motorcycles or around the desert property shrinks in anguish at the length of time it can take to head into civilization and do errands.

I, on the other hand, who can be a living dictionary and amateur detective all while producing a magazine, am used to the 12 hours of errands. In fact I prefer to pack every stop into one day rather than having to head out on another journey just a day or two later. So when he says he'll go with me to do the weekly errands, I sometimes cringe because I know we're not going to get everything done. Eight hours into the day he will say he's ready to go home.

However, recently a sick kid on my watch kept me from getting some much needed errands done and with the deadline staring me right in the face I wondered "just how long can we go without food?"

The guy-in-the-garage, motivated by some truck parts that were waiting for him in town, offered to do the grocery shopping so I could keep pounding out the pages.

Some of the stores on our route needed to be re-stocked with magazines as well, I mentioned to him.

No problem, he said, just make a list.

I helped get him ready to go. Bank deposit (because you might as well do the banking too if you're going into town), cell phone, debit card, cash and list of about six or seven places he was going to.

"Oh and do you have the ice chests and the gas can?" I asked.

"Yes," he said calmly as he headed out the door. And then while I was rushing out the door with the cold drink he forgot, I did the unthinkable. I attempted to add one more task.

"Oh, why don't you go ahead and pick up a new pair of jeans too?" I called out from behind him.

I can see it now as if it was happening all over again right in front of my face. And to tell the truth I can hardly keep from bursting out laughing.

If you've ever seen the post office scene in the *Grinch Who Stole Christmas* with Jim Carrey, you'll be able to picture exactly what happened.

It's the scene where the Grinch's dog has just forced him to save Cindy Lou Who from slipping into the gears of the package processing machine. Then as he heads for the door and is almost ready to make his escape she says "Thank you for saving me."

You can hear the sound of a screeching skid as he instantly comes to a stop and then very slowly turns around.

And that is exactly what happened when I mentioned the jeans. I'm sure I heard the dirt screeching he stopped so quickly. Then he turned around to look at me.

This guy who I have seen spend hours fabricating and machining one tiny little part to make something work better on a motorcycle gets totally overwhelmed at the thought of doing more than five or six errands in a day.

And while he didn't actually say it I could read the Grinch's next word in his mind: "Wrongo!!!"

So I smiled, waved good-bye and assured him that "yes, your cell phone is turned on already."

Don't want to overwhelm the guy because now it appears that almost anything I need while on deadline is not too much to ask. And getting my errands done and the fridge and cupboards restocked without ever leaving my desk made my day.

Chapter 12

Published March 2016

So there I sat at the intersection waiting to turn left. I had the misfortune of being the first vehicle at the light. Therefore I had a front row, and way-too-close-up, seat to the action. The disheveled man darted across the street and took up his post on the median to take advantage of all the cars stopped at the red light. He previously had been stationed at the corner, but when that light turned green and cars drove off he targeted the cars at the red light in the left-hand turn lane.

Thundering Trails, an Easter Egg Hunt & The Great Socialism Experiment

Yawning, bare foot, sporting a full leg tattoo and smoking a cigarette, the 20-something degenerate must have imagined himself something of a marketing genius. For his cardboard sign didn't have the usual "hungry, out of work" type message. No this guy was an original. His sign said "Dropped off by an alien, need a taco."

As I did my best to ignore him, "don't make eye contact" is a motto we frequently live by, I couldn't help but compare the activities of my day to his and his unkempt lazy partners who were stationed at every median in the intersection. At my desk at 6:45

that morning, I pushed hard on the deadline for this issue, knowing that at 1:45 I had to make a mad dash to town (two hour round trip) to do banking, groceries and get birthday supplies for the 10-year-old, be back in time to pick her up by 6, prepare a super fast easy dinner, spend an hour of family time and then back at the computer until at least midnight, the same quitting time I'd had the previous night.

But this guy who hasn't worked in who knows how long, maybe never, wants me to give him money for a taco.

I don't think so.

I have nothing against helping people in need. We regularly do that. We have devoted thousands of hours in the last few years to providing an off road camping adventure for kids who come from disadvantaged homes.

What I do have a problem with is helping people who are not helping themselves. At all. For instance the taco-loving alien. I was outraged when the car behind me handed the guy some money. Let's just encourage the "I-don't-need-to-work-I'll-just-beg-money-from-the-people-who-do-work" ethic, why don't we?!

While in the process of helping kids from at-risk homes at a Thundering Trails camp a few years ago I personally witnessed the concept of socialism and what a huge failure it is. In fact it was my own misguided idealism that caused the entire situation.

Whenever we have a camp that falls near Easter we do an Easter Egg hunt for the kids. The boys love these hunts as much as the girls. It can be challenging to hide a few hundred eggs without 12 rowdy kids knowing what you're doing. Since many of them are candy-filled and it's getting fairly warm in the desert around that time they can't be put out before the kids arrive at camp. So usually I'm up super early on Sunday morning (and that's after getting to bed around 1 or 2 a.m. because I was up late working on the camp poster) and I go to a part of the property where I don't think they'll see me if they happen to be early risers.

When the time came for the hunt during this particular boys' camp I wanted to make sure the eggs would be split fairly among them when the hunt was over. So I came up with what I thought was a great idea. I told the boys that there were enough eggs for each one of them to get 21 eggs. "You can find as many as you want, but after the hunt, be sure to count your eggs and if you have more than 21, share with someone who didn't get as many."

Sounded like such a wonderful idea. Until I saw how a few of the boys implemented that plan.

We were only minutes into the great Easter Egg Hunt of 2013 when I witnessed first-hand exactly why socialism, or being "fair" to everyone, does not work.

Anthony was super excited about the hunt and he took off like gangbusters and stayed on high speed the entire hunt, he

51

found more eggs than anyone and seemed to be having a fun time doing it. He didn't pass a single bush without checking to see if there was a colorful plastic eggs hidden in the depths of it.

While a couple of other obviously very unmotivated boys sauntered along hardly even glancing at the bushes they slowly passed by.

And if they didn't feel like trying hard, what difference did it make? They were going to get 21 eggs each even if they didn't put forth the effort to find a single egg.

Yet Anthony who's face was glistening with sweat as he gave 110% effort in the heat of the day would have to give up the majority of the eggs he found.

All because I thought the division of eggs should be fair.

Socialism. It does not work. Neither do half of the people who believe in it.

Chapter 13

Published May 2016

You couldn't actually say she was an off roader, but she was enthusiastic about the off roading other people did. She was a fan. A big fan of the sport. And one of *our* biggest fans.

She doesn't remember much, but on the occasions I visit her without the guy-in-the-garage I'll tell her "Steve couldn't be here today. He's working on motorcycles."

"Well of course!" she'll say with a chuckle and big smile. This lady who can barely remember her own name and not much else about her life has never forgotten the importance of motorcycles in our lives.

"I've never had a garage since I met my son-in-law," was one of her favorite sayings for decades as she fondly related tales of him filling her garage with off road toys of every type and size.

Now she doesn't remember she had a garage. Or a house.

She doesn't remember that if it wasn't for her there would never have been an *S&S Off Road Magazine.* In the early 1980's this very non-business-savvy lady was struggling to make a go of a typesetting business she had started on a shoestring budget that never grew past the daily struggle to survive. I logged in thousands of hours working for her without pay to help keep her head above water. While at the time that seemed like a sacrifice of love I have come to realize that in fact it provided the launch pad for us to start a small newsletter that we did not realize would grow into a popular magazine we would still be publishing 34 years later.

She loved driving the truck we bought for her about 10 years ago sporting *S&S Off Road Magazine* decals on all sides. She carried magazines with her and enjoyed immensely handing them out to anyone she encountered in parking lots or gas stations that she thought might be an off road enthusiast.

Summer 2015. Me, two sons, two grandkids and my mom.

She was driving that truck the night we got the midnight phone call from the CHP.

"Your mom was found driving on the wrong side of Interstate 8," the kind and compassionate voice related the words I had never wanted to hear.

She lived alone about two hours away from us and we had seen the signs of what could possibly be early dementia coming on during our bi-weekly visits in recent years.

Phone calls to a close associate of hers had reassured us that we didn't need to intervene yet. He had not seen any change in her. "Please call me when that time comes," I asked the trusted gentleman.

But before he was able to notice anything a sudden drastic turn for the worse took her miles away from her home to an area she never went to, heading into the mountains on I-8 driving east in the westbound lanes. The hand of God on her truck and the quick thinking CHP officers who responded to 9-1-1 calls kept her, as well as all other drivers on the freeway, safe that Saturday night one Christmas season a few years ago.

We had arrived at the time of life she had been dreading for years, suspecting this was a possibility, following in the footsteps of a couple of generations before her. She moved into our home two nights after that midnight phone call and we began an interesting and challenging time of multi-generational care-giving with a young granddaughter and aging mother depending on us to keep them safe and provide for their needs.

We continued to operate our off road camp for kids as well as the magazine and there were nights I laid awake long into the night with tears seeping out wondering what the future held and for how many years we could endure.

A little less than two years later with guidance and encouragement from close family members we moved my mom into an assisted living facility about an hour and a half away from our remote desert home.

Her needs had advanced to the stage that not only could we not leave her alone, the personal care she required would have been too humiliating for her to have extended family members help her with when we had to be out of town.

Without a doubt this was one of the hardest decisions of my life and one of the most difficult to follow through on.

She was, at that time, aware of the change, aware of the fact that she was not going to be living with us, and while she appeared to be in agreement, she too found the initial transition a difficult one.

I remember trying to paint a word picture for her in one of the early visits after her move to help her cope with the realities of dealing with difficult changes in our lives.

She was not in a wheelchair yet, and as we walked slowly around the facility together, she shuffled along with her walker. "Mom, do you remember when we moved while I was in 4th grade and I had to go to a new school?"

Yes, she said she remembered.

"Do you remember that I did not want to go to the new school and that I cried and cried and cried that first morning and you still made me go to school?"

She said she remembered.

I stopped walking and stared straight into her eyes to ask my final question. The one that would help her understand and accept this new challenge. The question that would help her to realize this was as hard for me as it had been for her all those years ago.

"Why did you make me do that when I didn't want to go to that new school?"

This gentle kind-hearted woman who throughout her life rarely raised her voice or uttered a harsh or rude word totally destroyed the point I was trying to make when she stared right back into my eyes and said bluntly "Because I knew you were going to do this to me someday!"

And in that instance as we both stared at each other and then started to laugh together, I knew it was going to be all right. We would both have many more tears to shed over the new arrangement, but we were going to be all right.

And nearly three years later in spite of continued and steady mental deterioration if I tell her "Steve can't be here today, he's working on motorcycles," it's always the same response.

Big smile. Chuckle. Then the ever faithful response "Of course he is!" reminds me that somewhere inside she remembers.

Chapter 14

Published June 2016

I remember when my dad died. Or I should say I remember when we found out he died.

A family member ran across it on the internet.

Ho-hum.

Not a great legacy to leave as a dad.

I could have cried. Some do I'm told. But my tears had all been shed years before. Thousands of tears. Maybe millions. For years. So I had none left to shed.

He had been gone less than a year when we made the discovery. My sister sent away for copies of his death certificate so we could find out something about his final days.

More out of curiosity I think than anything.

My dad as you can probably tell did not take being a dad very seriously. What he did take seriously was pursuing his own pleasures. Women. Alcohol. Gambling.

I will never forget the morning I woke up and his car was not in the driveway. I was 14. And that was that. The end of our family as I had known it.

Years went by and eventually we got over it. But to this day, my mom, even with her dementia I'm sure still holds a torch for the only love of her life. She went on to live a full life without him, maybe even better since it was no longer tainted by the ravages of alcoholism, but she never stopped loving him.

"It's my life, it doesn't matter what I do. My choices are my own," I heard another father say when confronted by his daughter about his alcohol consumption and lack of faithfulness to his family.

Oh but it does. It matters so very much. If you're living a lie, you're hurting others more than you might ever know. Maybe it's more than you want to know. Maybe if you knew exactly how much you're hurting others you wouldn't be able to continue the lie and so you have eyes only for what brings you pleasure and close your eyes to the sadness family and friends might be experiencing because of your choices.

I love the off road dads feature we run every June. I love the fact that while I wasn't blessed to grow up with an off road dad, thousands of kids are. And many off road dads out there impact

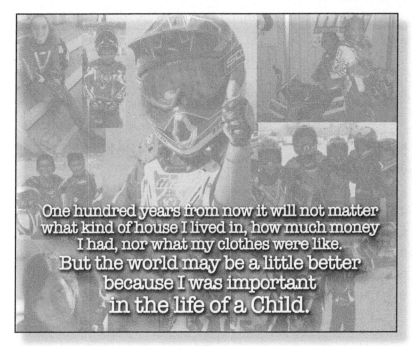

One hundred years from now it will not matter what kind of house I lived in, how much money I had, nor what my clothes were like. But the world may be a little better because I was important in the life of a Child.

kids far beyond their own. Neighbors, nephews, nieces, grandkids or even volunteering in capacities that impact kids unrelated or unknown to them.

You know for years I hung on to the hurt my dad caused. For years, even as a young adult I could find myself dwelling on the sorrow and giving in to the sadness, but one day a friend confronted me about that. It was rather embarrassing. We were at the monthly critique group of a writer's guild I was part of at the time and she spoke out in front of the whole group. "You need to let that go," she said of the hurt I had been writing about. I was embarrassed. Excruciatingly so. Then I was indignant. "She doesn't know," I thought. And as if she could read my mind, she said "My dad left our family when I was younger than you were."

She still doesn't know. I told myself. It's not the same for her. And for days I licked my wounds, now not only was I still angry/upset with my dad, I was upset with her as well for not understanding.

And then came the morning I woke up and realized. She was right.

And I got on with my life and never shed another tear over that man.

But lest you're like that man, living a lie so you can squeeze all the pleasure out of life you want, don't console yourself with the thought that "see, she got over it, my family will too," because it's not that easy.

I found that even to this day out of nowhere there are pangs of grief for the fact that the secret dream I always had even after I let go of the tears, would now never ever happen. That dream? To see my mom and dad reunited. To hear my dad say he was sorry. Or better yet, *show* he was sorry. It's not the words necessarily that are so important but the actions that can speak louder than words.

That day I heard he had died, I knew that my dream had died with him. And that was the saddest part of it all.

What about you? If you haven't been faithful to your family there is still time to change. And for those thousands upon thousands of faithful dads out there, my hat's off to you. You are changing the world. You are changing your family. You maybe have no idea how important everything you do is to the members of your family both immediate and extended. You have no idea how even the smallest things will stay in their memories forever. Getting up and going to work, coming home to share a meal. Enjoying a movie together, riding together. Even just being there to say good morning or good night. It doesn't even have to be something huge. Just being there.

One day you'll be gone. How do you want your family and friends to remember you? Do you want them to say "Wow, he really knew how to party!" or do you want them to say "Wow, he was there for us. He really loved us. All of us."

It's never too late to begin working on the legacy you want to leave.

A legacy that could, quite possibly, change the world. Or at least one child's world.

Chapter 15

Published August 2016

D o you want to drive?"
I cringe when I hear those words.

I knew how to drive when I met the guy-in-the-garage. I even had my driver's license to prove it, but just barely.

We married as teenagers and shortly after, he decided I needed to learn how to drive a stick shift. I don't recall him asking my opinion. At the time I hadn't been taught to ride a motorcycle yet either (that's another story), so the concept of clutches and gas pedals and gear shift levers was all rather foreign.

Over the years I discovered an interesting pattern of speech that occurred.

Shortly after I would hear the words "Do you want to drive?" the next phrase to leave his mouth after I had taken over the driving duties was usually something along the lines of "Well, don't kill us while you're doing it!"

Getting back to the stick-shift lessons: shortly after they began we planned a cross-country trip to visit grandparents.

He insisted I needed to help drive. Which I wouldn't have minded, except that we were taking the truck that he was in the process of teaching me to drive.

Let me explain my level of confidence in driving that truck. I had actually driven it alone a few times after he taught me. Unfortunately, it took me many extra miles to get to each of my destinations because I would carefully plan my trip so that I did not have to stop on any hills, or even gradual slopes. I made sure I had as few intersections to go through as possible, and preferred ones with stop lights rather than stop signs because at least I had a 50/50 chance of hitting the light green and not having to stop at all. It took so long to plan a trip that I probably could have reached my destination faster by walking.

So as we planned this trip I agreed to drive only on the highways and if we went through any towns he had to take over immediately so I didn't have to worry about stalling at every intersection.

He agreed.

But I didn't realize he was agreeing just to get me to shut up. Something I have realized now, decades later, happens frequently.

Things were going well on our trip. He seemed to be keeping to the agreement until we hit Gallup, New Mexico.

This was in the 1970's and the highway went right through town. A town that had a red light at every block for about a thousand blocks. These lights weren't timed so you could hit them all green either. They were timed so you would hit them all red.

"You're doing fine," he said. Which translated means keep driving because he isn't going to keep his agreement. If I didn't know how to work a clutch smoothly before I entered the town, I had about a thousand opportunities to practice before we got out of there.

A few years later we went motorcycle racing in Colorado, with another trip to visit grandparents in Kansas planned for afterwards. By then, I was pretty proficient with the clutch and that wasn't the problem. The driving problem this time was that at the race he broke several bones and was in no condition to help with the driving. He was determined to get to Grandma's house as soon as possible.

I drove and drove all night long. Whenever I suggested pulling over to rest, he would wake up out of his pain medicated daze and say "You're doing fine," which translates "keep driving!"

Thankfully we arrived safely and he was able to heal enough while we were there that he didn't have to tell me how fine I was doing all the way back to California. Instead he was able to do much of the driving.

I discovered the real meaning to his comment as years went by. "You're doing fine," really wasn't a way for him to express confidence in my driving. It was what he said when he was too tired to drive.

However exhausted he was though, he usually mustered up the strength to give me driving tips. You might call them friendly pointers. Although at times they really didn't seem so friendly.

For instance, once after another bout of motorcycle riding injuries, he was going stir crazy at home during the recuperation and asked me to drive him somewhere. He wasn't in the best of moods and was grumbling and complaining about not being able to do anything. We were sitting at an intersection and we were the first one at the red light with a long line of cars behind us. Just before the light turned green, he was griping because he wasn't even able to drive. He had me so flustered by then, that I popped the clutch without giving it enough gas and his reassuring comment as I attempted to restart the truck with horns honking was, "And apparently you can't drive either!"

We scrapped the "fun outing" and headed home.

Over the years I've driven him crazy when I'm behind the wheel of various vehicles from small trucks to a motorhome towing an enclosed trailer. But finally something happened that brought it all to a halt.

We were heading down the fairly narrow Banner Grade on our way to our desert home. I was driving through all the winding roads with huge motorhomes and trailers coming at us in the opposite direction and finally he said, in a somewhat exasperated voice: "You SCARE me driving on these roads!"

I couldn't respond because I was too busy concentrating and trying to stay on my side of the road.

It was silent for a minute or two and then he asked, "Do you scare yourself, too?"

"Actually, yes I do," I managed to admit.

He had me pull over at the very next turn-out and hardly ever asks me to drive for him anymore.

Chapter 16

Published October 2016

What are they doing there?" the guy grumbled.
"I didn't tell them they could park there!" responded
his equally unfriendly sounding teammate.

Without looking up I could feel several sets of eyes glaring our way.

I'll admit it. The guy didn't tell us we could park there. In fact he very emphatically told us we could not park there.

We parked there anyway.

The good 'ole boys club. Ever been a victim of it?

We leave early to get a good spot in the pits. Some race tracks this is easy. Others it's easier said than done.

Twice this year we've moved when told. Moved to a much less desirable spot.

We were determined this time we were going to get there early *again* and park where we wanted to park. That's the point of arriving early. You know what they say. The early bird gets the worm. Or in this case the prime parking spot.

What awaited us was a hassle that left us parked in a cubbyhole blocked in by others who may not have properly been taught how to share. But at least we were in the general area where we wanted to be.

Special message to the folks who tried to shoo us away: Try being polite next time. Try telling your whole group to man up and get there early or plan on parking on the outskirts.

But don't think you can cordon off an area big enough for multiple rigs just because one small truck was sent ahead to reserve the non-reserved spots. Or better yet ante up and buy the reserved spots available just across the way.

Sometimes there is such an air of "I belong you don't" that permeates the attitudes of some people. And believe me it's an attitude I detest.

Years ago we were parked in what we fondly referred to as "the old spot" in Ocotillo Wells. We had been camping in the same spot for probably 20 years or more. There was always evidence that someone else also used our favorite spot, but up until one dreaded weekend we had never gone to the desert at the same time.

Sure enough the time came and the interlopers showed up, most unwanted and in foul humor once they saw us in "their" spot. I can call them interlopers because I know that's what they called us (or worse).

I was in the motorhome reading. It was nightfall and the kids and most of the other adults were outside, some of them hanging around the campfire and others just goofing around in general. I had seen headlights shining into the motorhome so I knew someone else had pulled up. Then I decided that surely I really couldn't quite be hearing correctly when a few minutes later an angry woman's voice screamed out: "Do you know where you're parked?!!"

I don't even know what the folks in our group said in response, they were probably all as stunned as I was. Then I heard her screaming some more, "You're parked right in the middle of our track!!"

Wow, their track. Say, can I see the property deed naming you as owner of this spot? I didn't bother asking and I don't even remember how that particular weekend challenge ended, but I'm quite sure we weren't the ones who moved to a different location.

At least not that weekend.

We did decide in the interest of having future peaceful desert outings that we would find a new spot.

Sure enough the very next desert outing we discovered what we came to refer to as the "new old spot."

Things were going along well for quite a few trips until new interlopers arrived. Oh they didn't want our spot like the other troublemakers. These folks wanted our firewood. Said it was their's.

Now in all fairness I will say that it's quite possible at one time in the course of history the firewood may have belonged to them.

But when you leave your firewood unattended in the desert for weeks on end thinking that "your wood" will still be waiting in "your spot" when you finally decide to return to the desert, that is where the problem starts.

A couple of guys in our group had a fun time on every trip scouting the desert for bits and pieces of wood left behind by campers who don't know how to clean up their campsites. It benefits the desert, cleans it up, and benefits us. We get more firewood to add to our collection.

The conflict started when their kids stood on the outskirts of our camp and accused our kids of stealing their firewood. Again another unfortunate weekend when we happened to be in the desert as the same time as the undesirables.

While we attempted to ignore them, I vaguely remember that eventually the kids went and got their parents and the whole group of them came over to accuse us of stealing their firewood before they got out there.

And the line that really sticks out in my mind was that one of them hollered out "How long have you been coming to the desert?"

So the point being I'm to guess is that if they can offer concrete proof that they have been coming to this particular desert longer than we have (highly unlikely) that they had the authority and right to determine who owns the wood.

I'm not sure really their line of thinking but I do know that the next time we returned to that location we discovered the "bunker" our kids had built and played in for several years at that location had been torn down. We can only guess it was the kids who "owned" that firewood who did it.

It was once again time to find a "newer new old spot" in the hopes of having peaceful desert outings.

Keep all this in mind as you head *Back to the Desert* this year. If you haven't bought and paid for the sole right to use a plot of ground then just be glad when you arrive early enough to use it and try not to be a complete jerk if you get there and discover you just weren't early enough this time. Otherwise you ruin the outing for yourself and everyone you come in contact with.

Have an outstanding desert season! We thought it would never get here.

Chapter 17

Published December 2016

The week of November 6, 2016 was one of the most
fantastic weeks of my life.

It started out on Sunday with an amazing adventure at the
race track.

Then on that historic election day November 8, Donald Trump
was elected president in a victory that left the liberals stunned and
millions of Americans cheering for the incredible opportunity we
have to watch his plan play out in the coming months and years to
Make America Great Again!

And the week ended Saturday night November 12 with an
unforgettable 10th anniversary celebration for our Thundering
Trails off road camp for inner city kids.

It's not often that so many outstanding experiences happen in
the space of seven short days. I think I was walking on clouds all
week long and into the following week until I came crashing down
when I realized this issue was overdue to get to the printer and there
were hours and hours of work left to do!

But getting back to the way that week started. It's really a story
that goes back much further than last month. It's the story of a
dream the guy-in-the-garage has had for many years. Forty-eight,

to be exact. From the time he first started riding motorcycles at age 14, he longed to win a racing championship.

Over the years, as he attempted to pursue the goal, life kept taking him in different directions but the dream never went away.

In the fall of 2015 he was able to take a step in the direction of pursuing the goal. He acquired the motorcycle of his dreams, and according to the ad it was ready to race, a fresh build with only two races on it.

The guy-in-the-garage reading *The Big Blue M: The McMillin Racing Story* in the pits at Perris Raceway.

Little did we know at the time that was just the start of the challenges that awaited us.

A couple of test runs on it at the Camp Lockett track proved that this motorcycle would definitely be the one to give him a chance at a championship. The Perris Raceway flat track season would start in just a couple of months and just to give himself an additional edge, he decided to do some high performance work to the engine before the season started.

A decision that proved to be wise for all the wrong reasons. When Loren Duncan at Duncan Racing tore into the motor he found that not only was this engine not a fresh build, it was actually on its last legs with bits of metal in all the wrong places and a piston probably 10 years old. To make matters worse, the engine was not the year the seller said it was and the engine number had been removed so Duncan Racing was not able to determine exactly what year it was. That made ordering the correct replacement parts very

difficult.

In the meantime the weeks were ticking by and the first race of the season we had hoped to complete, from start to finish, was getting closer.

It almost seemed as if once again this would not be the year to pursue the goal.

Eventually with the help of Duncan Racing, Coyne Powersports and Hinson Clutch things were looking up and the rebuild was underway.

But not in time for the first couple of races. Thanks to fellow racers Jim Ottele and Woody Carlson who each loaned us a motorcycle, the guy-in-the-garage was able to get out on the track in the first few rounds and begin accumulating points in the 60+ Expert class.

The great day came when the engine was complete and one of the first races on it saw him win his first ever main event at Perris Raceway.

That was an exciting day. But he still needed to work hard at the points if he was to reach that coveted #1 spot and so he shipped his carburetor off to a guy who came highly recommended, anxious to get a few more horsepower. However that was about as effective as the "fresh build" we thought we were starting with. The first race after the modifications the bike didn't run right at all and the hope of gaining extra points was gone as in fact he went down in points after the "improvement."

Nearing the end of the season another main event win propelled him into the points lead, however a few more less desirable finishes whittled his lead down to only three points going into the final two rounds at the season ending double header.

It was a place he had never been before. Leading the points chase with a real chance to finish the year as the champion.

We arrived at the track early the day before the racing started and after getting the pit set up the guy-in-the-garage settled down to read a book we had recently received: *The Big Blue M: The McMillin Racing Story.* It's a thick book with well over 500 pages, and it's highly likely that book had a very real impact on the final outcome of our racing that weekend.

For the recurring theme throughout the book is the motto that the late Corky McMillin, patriarch of the McMillin Racing Family, lived by: "Never give up!" The book is filled with encouraging stories about Corky living out that motto in daily life whether it was his business or his racing.

Before the weekend was over it would be the encouragement that the guy-in-the-garage would have to grasp and live by if he were to have a chance to reach his goal.

Saturday night he went into the main event with a three point lead but a disappointing finish saw him roll off the track having lost four points to his challenger who now led by one.

It was a long night and the look in his eyes and the slump of his shoulders had me fully expecting that he wouldn't even race the next day. However early the next morning he disappeared for awhile and no one in our pits knew where he was. He returned later with renewed enthusiasm and a new plan. "Never give up," was resonating in his thoughts all night long and that morning when he had a chance to meet with a real flat track expert he welcomed the suggestions that this time he knew he could trust.

A start to finish win in the heat race proved the modifications were spot on and when the riders rolled to the start line for the main event they knew that the 12 race championship series had come down to the final race. The winner would be the 2016 60+ Expert champion.

They both were equally determined to win and that was evident as they raced the entire eight laps often side by side and exchanging the lead multiple times, but with a lap and a half to go the guy-in-the-garage pulled ahead and held the lead all the way to the checkered for the championship.

The tears in his eyes when he got back to the pits were of gratitude to the people who had helped him and the thrill of the sweet victory he'd waited 48 years to experience.

It's quite a principle to live by: Never ever give up.

Chapter 18

Published February 2017

I don't ride. Not much anyway. Maybe take my quad out on our desert property once or twice every couple years.

But I'm madly in love with a guy who does ride. The guy-in-the-garage. When he's not in his shop working on his motorcycles he might be out riding one of them. He tries to ride two to three times a week.

He was riding the day I met him. I was 16 and lived across the street from Brown Hill, a popular riding area for the local hot shoes.

That's how I first heard about him. Other kids in the neighborhood talked about this crazy motorcycle riding nut. And I figured this nut must need a girlfriend.

But the fact is the topic today isn't really about the guy-in-the-garage at least not the one I'm normally writing about. It's about all the other guys in garages across the nation. The guys who, like this one I'm married to, are passionate about their motorcycles. Or maybe another type of off road vehicle. It's a passion that runs so deep it's as vital to them as the blood that flows through their veins.

It's their life.

In the decades we've been together I've discovered a sad fact about off road marriages and that is that not all married guys who are passionate about riding have a spouse who fully and completely supports their love of motorcycles.

In fact in my years of observing this I have categorized wives in four different ways:

A. Those who love riding as much as the guys;

B. Those, like me, who don't ride but wholly and completely support the riding passion of their husbands;

C. Those who don't mind that their husband rides but really don't want anything to do with it and won't go to the desert or the track with them; and

D. Those who may occasionally tolerate their riding but view it as a very low priority, almost to the point that the husband has to resort to lying to be able to pursue his passion; or worse has to give it up completely.

So today I'm speaking to and about the wives who fall into the letter D category.

What do you have to give up if you move into category B or maybe even A? Some money missing from the bank account? Some activities of your own there isn't time for? Some projects around the house going undone? That's most likely the worry and it's possible those things may very well happen. But if those things happen, is that really the end of the world? Or the end of all happiness for all time? Maybe you might feel it's the end of your happiness but have you taken into account it might just lead to the beginning of your husband's true happiness?

Let's look at what else you have to lose. The arguments. The lying. The sneaking around. The lack of enthusiasm on his part, the lack of joy and happiness as he's been forbidden – yes forbidden since some wives actually wield that much power and authority in the home – to pursue his passion.

A passion that is not unique just to your husband, but one that is shared by thousands, even hundreds of thousands across this nation and around the world. Maybe even millions if you take into account all of the generations who have gone before us.

The April 2011 edition of Smithsonian Magazine writes: "A century ago, Americans fell in love with speed. While the Wright Brothers flew overhead and Model T's rolled off Henry Ford's assembly line, the new sport of motorcycle racing began drawing large crowds bent on celebrating a piston-powered future."[1]

Unfortunately mixed in with this rich history of motorcycle loving fanatics there is also a history of the type of wife who felt it her bound duty to prevent the pursuit of the passion.

In this same article we read about Ashley Franklin Van Order, a livery worker who loved motorcycles so much that in 1911 he relocated from Illinois to Southern California so he could ride his motorcycle year-round.

"Van Order took a job selling Harley-Davidsons and began riding competitively, but his racing career was cut short soon afterward by an accident, followed by an ultimatum. 'His wife, Lilly, told him that if he ever rode again, she was out of there,' says Van Order's grandson."[2]

He turned to photography to fulfill his motorcycle passion and eventually amassed the most complete photographic history of early motorcycle racing from the early 1900's in existence.

But how sad that within just a few years of motorcycles and motorcycle racing being invented, there were already wives interfering in the pursuit of the passion for their husbands.

My goal in life in the very early days was to be the wife in Category A. In our dating years and early married life, I imagined myself riding often and riding well, reaching the skill level that would allow me to enjoy rides with the guy-in-the-garage. I imagined myself racing and winning races. But after a number of years of attempting to reach this goal I discovered something else. My imagination was much more adventurous and courageous than my actual self was. And finally I reached a point where I could comfortably admit to myself and others that I was really a big chicken and my greatest joy came from supporting the guy-in-the-garage in his riding passion and even more fun, watching him when he is racing.

On Christmas Day we had a couple of young adult visitors who dropped in at our desert home for Christmas breakfast after a morning ride. The topic came up about girlfriends and motorcycles. "Do what you want and just lie to them," was the advice one had received from his boss in the event you have a girlfriend or wife who doesn't see the value in a day spent riding.

Surprisingly when I told the boys I had a couple of pieces of advice for them about marriage, they actually seemed interested in hearing what I had to say.

First, don't ever lie to your wife and second, don't marry someone you would have to lie to about motorcycles. They received the advice enthusiastically.

We finished breakfast, they drove off with their muddy bikes in the back of a muddy truck, stomachs full and a host of wonderful Christmas memories revolving around motorcycle riding in the desert filling their hearts. The hope is whatever the future holds for them in the way of relationships it will include a love of motorcycles that doesn't have to be hidden or denied.

Yes, I'm madly in love with a guy who rides. And madly in love with his motorcycles too. Because his motorcycles are his life. How could I not love them if I love him the way I do?

It's the big question of the day. And if you're a wife D, I encourage you to set a goal this year to move up to category B. You might just discover a new joy in life you never knew existed.

Chapter 19

Published April 2017

Yeah?!"

That was how he answered the phone.

Why is it I suddenly felt like hanging up on him?

"What do you need?" followed the impatient "Yeah?" when I didn't respond.

Unlike the good old days when a caller had no idea who was calling them I knew that he knew it was me. So hanging up on him just wasn't an option at this point.

"Uh, can you talk?" I muttered something along those lines or possibly something else equally as annoying to a guy who I later found out, had just extricated himself from the bowels of the current vehicle he was working on in time to run over to the workbench and grab the phone before he missed the call.

"I'm trying to get some work done," he said. "What do you want?"

By this time I had completely forgotten what I wanted. Well at least what I had originally wanted when I called him. I knew without a doubt that what I now wanted was to not only hang the phone up on him but to slam it down in the cradle. Except the most satisfaction you can get with hanging up on someone now is to press the end button really hard. Not nearly as effective as slamming a handset down. Not nearly as loud either.

So there I sat in my office, at my desk working, trying to think of something invaluable to tell him or ask him so I didn't have to actually say that he had me so rattled I now couldn't remember what I called him for.

In the good old days when he worked in a garage connected to the home office I could just stroll through the garage door, see that it wasn't a good time to talk, and stroll right back to my desk.

Not so nowadays. His shop was far enough away from the house that we had to resort to phone calls to communicate.

The funny thing about the phone lines. They work well when it's an incoming call to the office from the shop. They are answered pleasantly every time. Even when the calls come at the rate of 2-4 an hour. Important requests come through like, "I left my phone book on my desk up there, can you look a number up for me?" or "I forgot the parts on the back porch for this project, are you coming down this way soon?" Oh, here's a really good one. "We're back from riding, can you bring down some

Mountain Dew and banana bread?"

Since I'm not easily capable of shrugging off a major indiscretion such as being spoken to rudely on the telephone I couldn't just drop it and get back to work. I felt the need to rant and rave to myself about how I am so nice that I would never answer the phone like that when he calls me. I told myself that even if he calls three times in a row, every single time I answer the phone politely and help with whatever he needs or wants. I told myself that I wouldn't soon forget this improper treatment over the phone. I told myself so many things about that 2 minute phone call that I wasted probably 30 minutes, 15 times the amount of time that had actually been spent on the phone.

And that's when it occurred to me.

Probably the very sight of my number showing up on his Caller ID strikes fear into his heart. Fear of how many minutes he is going to have to listen to me rant and rave about whatever current issue has me up in arms. How many minutes of his time will I take up giving him the complete and lengthy history of my thought processes that led me to the decision that I needed his input on a certain topic.

Unlike his calls to me:

Him: "Can you get me this, that or the other thing?"

Me: "Yes."

Him: "Thanks. Good-bye."

Under a minute most calls.

Compared to my calls to him:

"Me: You know I was sitting at my desk working on the subscription renewals because I'm way behind on getting those done and I haven't had any time to work on them in the last month or so because of how hectic our schedule has been. So while I was working on the subscription renewals, I ran across the name of a guy you used to work for and I remembered when we lived in Chula Vista and you worked with him all the time and it made me curious if you have talked with him lately and do you think I should send him a renewal notice after all?

Him: Uh...

Me: Oh and actually that's not really why I called, his subscription isn't up for renewal yet, so you have some time to think about that. But the reason I actually called was because I was wondering if you've heard if it's going to be raining or windy this weekend because I was wondering if we should still go ahead and plan outdoor activities for camp or if we should have indoor activities?

Him: Uh . . .

Me: Well, you know what? I think I'll just plan activities for both indoors and outdoors so we'll be ready no matter what the weather is like.

Him: Ok.

Me: So how is everything going down there? What are you working on? Are you getting a lot done?

And now I'm understanding why on a busy day of working on a frustrating project the ringing phone, that hopefully is the motorcycle shop calling to say they have located the hard-to-find part, turns out to be a wife who most likely has way too much to say can be slightly annoying.

Did I say slightly? That may be an understatement.

I'm starting to realize that when my number shows up on the Caller ID it's a wonder he answers the phone at all.

Chapter 20

Published June 2017

What kind of a person does something like this? Sees something they don't like and without knowing anything about the history of it, without caring about the thousands of people and generations of families who have cherished the landmark, they demand its removal.

And what kind of laws do we have where that is all it takes? One person doesn't like it. Down it comes.

And is it some small coincidence that though the complaint was made in January in the midst of one of the busiest off road desert seasons in years, that plans were not put into place to actually remove it until the end of desert season? When no one is around to witness the removal? Coincidence? I think not.

The year was 1966. The war in Vietnam was raging. The anti-war movement was gaining steam. But the stranglehold of political correctness had not yet caught our nation or our state in its death grip.

A small town rural community devastated at the loss of one of their own young men killed in action in the far away war that now seemed much too close to home found a way to bring comfort to everyone. To mom and dad. Sister, nephew, friends and neighbors.

Thus was the start of the Ocotillo Wells Memorial Cross that thousands have treasured and generations have seen standing high on the hill at the airport in the small desert community that has come to be temporary home to hundreds of thousands of off road enthusiasts over the past five or six decades.

Elmo Robison, the last rural sheriff in San Diego County, lived across the street from the site of the cross erected not only in his son's memory, but also that of two other cherished members of the community that had been lost near the time of his son's passing in 1966. Elmo certainly knew the law. In the 51 years the cross stood its ground high atop the airport hill, certainly hundreds of others with a legal background saw the cross standing and no one had a problem with it.

Until January 2017. That was when one person complained to the Public Works Department of the County of San Diego and according to the County spokesperson it only takes one complaint about a religious symbol on government property and it has to be removed. As I write this, a battle is underway to prevent the cross from coming down, but the last we've heard from the County is that it will be removed.

While surrounded by the Ocotillo Wells SVRA the land the cross actually sits on is owned by the County of San Diego. However they can't do anything without permission from the FAA. The county spokesperson said they sought permission from the FAA to release that portion of land so the cross could remain without being on government land. The FAA denied the request.

What this boils down to is State and Federal laws that defy the wishes of thousands while granting overwhelming power to one person who decides they don't like something.

Crosses have been used as memorials for centuries around the world. In the year 1290 the King of England erected a series of thirteen monuments topped with crosses to commemorate the loss of the love of his life Queen Eleanor. Three of these monuments are still standing today. It is written of the King: "Edward was desperately saddened and shut himself away to mourn. He wrote: 'Living I loved her dearly and I shall never cease to love her in death.'"[1]

In New Zealand roadside crosses not only memorialize the loss of cherished life, but they have actually saved lives. The long-standing tradition of placing crosses at the scene of a fatal accident grew to include thousands of crosses throughout New Zealand and a noticeable reduction in traffic fatalities. The cross movement started in 1990 with a group of friends who were concerned about their children driving on the dangerous highways. Together the families erected 53 crosses over the next few weeks. The cross movement was not without detractors but enough people were in favor of it that it caught on and was so successful that the death toll began to drop. "By the end of 2000 the death toll was down from 600 to 425, despite a substantial increase in road usage over the five years since the campaign began. This was the lowest road toll in 36 years."[2]

In 2001 the New Zealand Police in conjunction with their traffic safety agency ran a full page ad on Mother's Day showing a white cross adorned with flowers and encouraging safe driving on the holiday weekend.

For many years the Ocotillo Wells Memorial cross could be seen and treasured by Elmo Robison and his wife as it stood high on a hill across the street from their home. They took comfort in this visible memorial tribute to their son who gave his life in service to our country.

Tom Lemmon, the nephew of Robison, was only 7 years old in 1966 and remembers his Uncle Jim as the "uncle every boy wanted." Tom lost his only uncle when he was killed in action and to this day takes comfort in seeing the memorial across the street from the family home that eventually was passed on to him.

But the fact that crosses have a historical significance dating back centuries around the world to remember the dead, that particular memorial and all it means to thousands of visitors to the desert doesn't matter because one person is offended by it.

What kind of a person is that?

Footnote: *After nearly a two year battle, on December 1, 2018 American Legion Post 853 purchased the land the cross was erected on and saved the memorial.*
https://www.legion.org/honor/244067/legion-helps-save-vietnam-veteran%E2%80%99s-memorial-removal

[1] http://www.timetravel-britain.com/articles/history/eleanor.shtml
[2] https://www.nzgeo.com/stories/roadside-crosses-a-memorial-and-a-message/

Chapter 21

Published August 2017

There are two things about me the guy-in-the-garage simply cannot tolerate. One is my driving, especially when it's his truck and two, is the way I break up ice.

So the first might be fairly self-explanatory, but the ice? Who could know something so seemingly simple could drive a man mad?

We live a long way from the grocery store. And on a hot summer day in the desert, it seems even longer. So every trip involves taking one to three ice chests for carting home groceries. Which means bringing home 20 to 50 pounds of ice to keep the ice cream and other various food items nice and cold.

The ice, as you might imagine, melts a little on the way home, and then when it gets back into the freezer it tends to turn into one giant block of ice instead of hundreds and hundreds of perfectly formed ice cubes.

The problem starts when I need some of those perfectly formed ice cubes and our ice bin is empty. Now usually the guy-in-the-garage is the one to keep it filled up, but occasionally I want ice and it's empty. I don't have a problem filling it myself. The problem comes if he happens to be anywhere in hearing distance of a 10 pound chunk of ice being banged around in the kitchen. Because I can guarantee you, no matter how I do it, or where I do it, he will not be happy about it. Just something about me and a frozen bag of ice really annoys him.

It's gotten to where I cringe if I realize I need ice and he is anywhere within a half mile radius of me and the freezer with the frozen bag of ice.

Okay, I understood finally, why it annoyed him that I would slam the bag of ice against the kitchen floor. I did notice the dog laying on the kitchen floor and I did finally realize that okay, probably some of that dog hair is getting on the bag of ice and then up on the counter and then who knows where else? Okay, just why did he have to wait so long to tell me he really had a reason for being annoyed about that.

So, next time I break up the ice in his hearing range, I'm doing it on the kitchen counter, so I don't get dirt from the floor on the bag. "What are you trying to do? Break the kitchen tiles?" he kindly asks. Did I say kindly? I think I misspoke.

Next time, I break up the ice on the kitchen table. "You can't do it right on the table like that," he says, "You have to put some padding down so you don't damage the table."

Okay, lest you're starting to think I deliberately wait until he is watching to break the ice, that's not it at all. He will be nowhere around. Nowhere! And like magic, if I start breaking open the ice, he appears. I don't know how he does it.

So the next time he is getting ice, I watch. I observe. I decide that I am now going to do it exactly like he does it. Exactly! He won't have one thing to complain about. Because it will be his method of breaking up ice that I will use.

And sure enough, the day came. He was sitting at the table eating lunch when I needed ice. Not wanting to disturb him, I figured this wouldn't be a problem because I was going to do it exactly like he does it. I get out the placemat he uses. I doubled it up like he does. Then I start banging the ice and what do you think happens? He stands up, takes the bag out of my hand and says "That's why the plant is falling over!" as he points to the granddaughter's cactus plant that is resembling the Leaning Tower of Pisa in a makeshift terrarium on the table.

What?! I want to scream. But I'm not a screamer. So I very quietly say "That is exactly how YOU do it." He said "Well, I guess I never noticed the plant falling when I'm doing it."

So now if I want ice and there is no ice, I have a new plan. I go without.

That seemed to solve my ice problem at home, but then there are those times we are on the road and I happen to have some responsibility connected to bags of ice.

Take the time a few years ago at the Sand Sports Super Show in Costa Mesa, California. At the end of the show, the guy-in-the-garage was out at the trailer loading up all the vintage bikes and I was cleaning up the last of the items in the booth when I noticed that our ice chest had leaked water all over the floor.

Along comes our awesome building manager Rocky and even after working the long, long show hours, in his always friendly voice he says, "Don't worry about it, I'll clean it up."

I really didn't want to leave that mess for him and I told him so.

He started laughing. "Oh, this is nothing!" he said. "You should have seen what a lady did last year." And he laughs even harder. "She dumped the whole entire ice chest out all over the floor. Ice and water went everywhere! You should have seen it! It was a mess!"

I just looked at him without laughing. "I did see it," I told him without laughing. "That was me."

He laughed louder. "That was YOU?! I completely forgot."

I surely didn't forget. I remember that Rocky helped me carry the last of the items from our booth that day while the ice and water was trickling along the showroom floor.

When we got out to the trailer he said to the guy-in-the-garage, who was getting ready to go check our booth one last time: "You don't want to go back in there. Trust me!"

And then he wandered off chuckling, back to the river of water and ice awaiting him in Building 14.

And thankfully for me he saved my neck from the guy-in-the-garge who would have had one more ice incident to give me never-ending grief about.

Chapter 22

Published September 2017

Remember back in our school days and the constant fun of passing notes to friends? Besides the simple fun of "chatting" with friends instead of paying attention to school work, there was the thrill of doing it without getting caught.

All these years later I finally really understand the problem with passing notes in school. It's distracting, disruptive and downright rude.

Unfortunately we've taken it to a whole new level with text messaging.

Sure, it's convenient. Easy. Even fun to get messages. But why are messages coming through on a phone so much more important than the person we're talking to face to face? Important enough that we have to sneak a glance. Or maybe you've been in a conversation where the other person does more than sneak a look, they full on give all their attention to reading the text, responding, laughing out loud or commenting about something, and the present face-to-face conversation is totally gone. Out the window.

Oh for a teacher to hand out consequences for this modern day note-passsing indiscretion.

Reading texts during a face-to-face social encounter may be rude but the text addicts take it to a whole new level, risking their very lives and the lives of others because they can't resist the urge while they're driving.

"Road fatalities have increased significantly in the past few years. The National Safety Council (NSC) found that the number of fatalities on U.S. roads rose by 14 percent since 2015, the largest two-year increase in five decades."[1]

Wisconsin mother and aunt Kari Milberg was one of thousands who text and drive. "What can it hurt?" she may have said if someone had called her on it. "It won't happen to me," is probably what most people, even people reading this column may think. "I'm just doing it real fast."

"Prosecutors say when Milberg crossed the center line with five children in the car, she was texting -- using the phone app Facebook Messenger."[2]

Those text messages that were too important to wait until later, took the lives of her 11-year-old daughter and two five-year-old nieces. It would be two years before the criminal ordeal was over as she was charged with three counts of vehicular homicide. Ultimately she was acquitted after the defense attorney convinced the jury her worn out tires on a rainy and snowy road caused the

accident and not the texting. The final message on her phone was sent 19 seconds before the 911 call was received. The defense attorney also suggested it could have been the 11-year-old daughter texting. The mother says she remembers nothing as does the recipient of the text messages.

A google search for distracted

driving brings up pages and pages of tragic news reports about families torn apart due to the deaths of children or parents or both killed because of texting. There is even a website dedicated to the modern day tragedy: www.distracteddrivingkills.ca - don't miss the opportunity to check out this site and read the stories of people who have lost loved ones needlessly.

Sadly in many of the reports it's the innocent passengers or people in other vehicles who are killed as a result of the texting.

If risking your own life isn't enough to get you to stop texting while driving, how about knowing you could be the cause of multiple other people dying?

And what about those of us who are expecting someone at the race track or on an off road outing? We know they're on the way, but they haven't arrived yet. So what do we do? We text and ask "what are you doing? are you almost here?" Even if you're not the one driving and texting you're enabling and encouraging someone who is driving to risk lives just because we think we need to know where they are.

Is it uncool to worry too much about texting and driving? Is it being overly fanatical? Is it excessive worrying about something that most likely isn't going to happen?

Ask these questions of the families of the nearly 3500 people killed in 2015 Ask the 391,000 injured in 2015 due to distracted driving if they think its being fanatical to worry about texting and driving.

Next time you're tempted to send a text or read an incoming one while driving, first ask youself:

Is it worth dying for?

[1] https://www.cmtelematics.com/press/new-data-cambridge-mobile-telematics-shows-distracted-driving-dangers/

[2] http://www.kare11.com/news/crime/trial-begins-monday-for-mom-accused-of-distracted-driving/256640091?1467001166929

Chapter 23

Published October 2017

Everything I need to know about people and life I learned handing out magazines at the Sand Sports Super Show recently.

When you pose the same question to 6,000 different people interesting patterns start to form. Entire personalities are revealed in the way people respond to the question: Would you like a magazine?

For instance, and let's just get this totally rude one out of the way right off the bat. "Would you like a magazine?" I politely ask of a couple of people strolling by the booth. They are both looking right at me, definite eye contact there, admittedly looking somewhat bored and not the least bit interested in what I'm saying.

And what really annoys me is they don't even acknowledge that I've asked them a question, don't respond at all, not even a grunt, no nod or shake of the head. Then in the same bored fashion they look away and keep on strolling.

My psychological analysis of this personality type is one of two things: They are most likely rude and self-absorbed people who don't feel they need to be even a little bit polite to someone who has so obviously spoken directly to them.

Secondly it could be, they are easily overwhelmed and the massive amount of activity in the building has them so confused they don't even know someone has spoken to them. I tend to believe it's the rude analysis. Thankfully very few people responded like that.

My very favorite response and one that we can all learn from is the person who responds with enthusiasm.

I had this happen a number of times and it's incredibly encouraging and really good inspiration for all of us to live life just like these people. Their faces light up with a smile that reaches all the way up to their eyes. "Yes I'd love one!" they enthusiastically respond as they reach out and take the magazine. "Thanks so much!" they'll say or sometimes even "Can I have an extra one for my friend?"And they continue on their way fully enjoying every moment of life and all of the experiences awaiting them at the Sand Show, and most likely anywhere else they go.

Then you have the sheep. The ones who follow the crowd. A big group coming by, and the first person says yes and takes ones. I love that because then every person in the group will take one. I cringe when the first person says "no thanks" because every person behind them also says "no thanks." The awesome thing too about the group where everyone takes a magazine is then people come flocking from all around, even the ones who weren't in the original group because they want what everyone else is getting.

But what I love the most about the sheep people is that one person who will break from the pack. You have the group where the leader says no and all the rest mimic him, but then, you discover someone who thinks for themselves. A person near the back of the pack says "I'll take one!" Yes! That rarely happens, but what that tells me about that person is they don't just do something because that's what everyone else is doing, they evaluate the opportunity and make their own decision and go for it.

Men generally aren't willing to carry the magazine. They want it but they bring along wives, girlfriends or sons and daughters to carry all the free show goodies for them. And the family members good naturedly haul the freebies in bags and backpacks and also seem to be enjoying the show as well. My psychoanalysis says good family dynamics going on there. Lots of support and caring for one another in that family.

Then you have the wives/girlfriends standing alone in the middle of the aisle, looking bored while their significant other is enjoying a nearby vendor booth.

"Would you like a magazine?" I ask them because it's my policy to ask that question of every person in my immediate vicinity whether they're looking at me or not, whether they look interested or not, whether I think they'll take the magazine or not. That's my policy. Ask the question. And sometimes they'll take it, but more than likely the bored woman standing alone won't take it, she'll politely refuse and usually looks like she can't imagine why I would even ask her.

What I can't imagine is why are you there if you can't even show a little enthusiasm for the sport that your significant other is obviously so passionate about? Probably because they're hoping they'll get out of there soon and go do something she likes to do. I'm not a marriage counselor but I'd say that's definitely not an indication of great family dynamics there.

Probably the funniest couple passing by our booth was the husband/wife who both insisted on having their own copy because as the husband said "She won't share with me!" While walking off I heard her say "You're the one who won't share!" As long as they both read the magazine it makes no difference to me whether they share or not!

Finally, one of my policies is to politely never accept a "no" response. I continue holding the magazine up facing them so they can clearly see the enticing cover shot and it happens over and over again. Someone who has said no and walked on, comes back to the booth and says "Yes, I will take one after all!"

And that teaches us that it's never too late to reconsider if we've made a wrong decision and do whatever needs to be done to make it right.

Who would have thought you could learn so many lessons about life just handing out a magazine?

Here's to 35 more years of publishing. Welcome back to the desert! We thought the summer would never end!

Chapter 24

Published February 2018

We have two time zones in our little world. That world that consists of our home, office and shop.

You probably didn't know our desert property where we live, work and play, was so large that it extended out of one time zone into another. But that's the truth, never mind that you can walk from the home/office to the shop in less than five minutes. The fact remains, it's in a different time zone.

The guy-in-the-garage calls me up and says "Can you come down here and help me for a minute?"

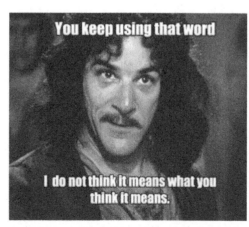

I'm working on my own deadline up here, but I always like to help, so I quickly, or fairly quickly, well, okay, as soon as I finish up several more things I am trying to do, hurry down to help him for a "minute."

"Sit on this bike," he says. "I need to adjust the chain. It will just take a minute."

So I throw a leg over the current project bike he's got going and I sit there and although I don't have a watch on and I don't have a cell phone with me and the clock in his shop is behind me, I'm somehow quite sure I've been sitting there for longer than a minute. In fact probably longer than 10 minutes.

He's making some adjustments and muttering to himself and then he gets up and heads across the shop and says "I have to make a few changes and then I can adjust it." He looks back at me. "It will just take a minute," he says.

I wonder if I should laugh. It seems like it would be rude because I think he really believes what he is saying. By this time I'm pretty sure I've been down there almost 20 minutes. So I sit on the bike staring off into space and mentally noting the order of things on my to-do list and what I need to be working on as soon as I am done helping him and trying hard not to grow frustrated.

Finally he comes back to the bike I am still sitting on (I should have brought a book to read) and says, "Okay, I think now I have it right." I hear him tinkering with some tools as he's doing something I can't see and then he says it again. "Okay, this will just be a minute and then you can go. I'm sorry, I know you have a lot of work to do. But it should be just a minute."

Okay, so how do you not laugh out loud at something like that?

But you know, I'm just the polite type of person that I have to laugh to myself because I can tell he really believes what he is saying when he asks me to help him for a minute.

It sure seemed like about an hour had passed by the time I headed back up to the office to try to remember what pressing deadline I needed to get back to now that my "minute" of helping him was over.

But when I want to show him something on my computer that he needs to approve of or make a choice about or maybe even laugh at, whatever the reason, big problems come up regarding the amount of time he is willing to give to me. If there is something that exists somewhere in the bowels of my computer or that I and only I can access online (meaning he has no clue how to find it), he expects it to be on the screen instantly the very second he steps up to my desk.

And if it isn't there and I make the terrible awful no-good mistake of saying "It will just be a minute," that's it. I've lost him. He's gone, shaking his head, saying "I'll be back when you really have it ready for me to look at."

This guy, who has without qualm, expected me to sit for hours on end (slight exaggeration) waiting while he does things in the shop to get ready for the instant that he will need my help, will not wait 60 seconds (okay, sometimes it's a tiny bit longer) for me to show him something. I do have to admit my computer knows him. My computer knows the instant he steps near my desk to thoroughly hide every single file I need to access to find what he wants to see. The internet will freeze up and nothing will work when he steps near it.

And the guy-in-the-garage won't just step away quietly, he will let me know that I have imposed on his valuable time by expecting him once again to wait and wait and wait.

But it finally occurred to me. Maybe we don't operate in different time zones and maybe the reason he walks away is because he knows when someone says "it will be just a minute," that in all reality, it could be 30 minutes or more.

And he is not now and has never been capable of patiently waiting for anything.

I can't count the miles we have driven out of our way to avoid sitting in traffic or stopping for road construction. Even if it takes longer to get to our destination, in his mind it was quicker, because he was constantly on the move and not sitting still.

Like the time we went out for dinner and drove away from five different restaurants because of long lines.

An hour later when we finally got to eat I casually mentioned that we would have eaten sooner if we had waited at the first place we went to. But apparently that wasn't the point.

"I don't wait in line to eat," was all he said. And since I really enjoy eating with him, I don't wait in lines either. I ride around in the truck with him.

Tonight while working late to meet the printing deadline for the magazine, he offered to make dinner.

"It's ready," he called out in no time at all.

"I'll be there in a minute," I said and surprised both of us by really showing up in a minute.

"Oh, I thought you were going to keep on working and just let our dinner get cold," he said as I entered the kitchen.

My mind quickly raced back over 40 years, mentally calculating how many cold dinners we have eaten because of shop projects that he couldn't pull himself away from.

"Those sound like fighting words," I thought and started to say so. But the silly grin on his face reminded me, what's the use?

It's how we've always done it and it works. I wait. He doesn't.

Chapter 25

Published March 2018

She would go to her grave hating carrots because of the kids teasing her in school for her bright red hair. They called her carrot-top. Even with the passing of eight decades she had not forgotten.

Bullies were around in the 1930's, but school shootings not so much, in spite of the fact that guns were readily available. This was an era when parents dealt with disciplinary problems with a visit to the woodshed.

These kids grew up to parent their children with the same methods. Spankings, grounding, getting sent to their rooms.

Yet today's parenting philosophy seems to almost ridicule the displinary styles of days-gone-by.

Sitting through some parenting conferences hosted by a social services agency recently I heard a leader state matter-of-factly that "our parents were doing their best but they didn't really know what proper methods of training and discipline are."

Then she went on to disparage grounding, spanking and sending a child to their room. The theory is spanking makes a child violent, sending them to their rooms causes them to feel isolated.

I pondered the fact that while the kids of my generation and earlier were raised by this method that supposedly causes kids to be violent and leads to other trauma, for all those theories, we sure weren't shooting up the students and teachers and we didn't have to have policemen assigned to schools.

It was an era when the schools had strict dress codes and we called all adults Mr. and Mrs. Kids were to be seen and not heard and we didn't just break into the adult's conversations, we were raised to be respectful and obedient and if not there were quick and effective discplinary measures enforced.

We had a healthy fear of parents, teachers and people in positions of authority.

Ask former Sheriff's Deputy Ben Fields how an unruly child can destroy a life. She was a 15-year-old high school student in South Carolina who didn't want to put her cell phone away when the teacher told her to. She had no healthy fear of the school administrator who was brought in to insist that she put the cell phone away. She still refused.

That was when the administrator determined it was time to call in law enforcement and she summoned the school resource officer.

This young lady still defiantly refused to surrender her phone, and the

Damn it, Mom! I've told you a hundred times... There is no way to 'pause' an online game!

situation escalated when Deputy Fields told her he would have to arrest her for refusing to comply and causing a school disturbance. Rather than go with him peacefully, she locked her legs around the legs of the desk chair and refused to budge as he attempted to physically remove her. In her vigorous attempt to prevent him from removing her, the desk tipped over and when he finally separated her from the desk it appeared she had been thrown to the ground. Friends of the unruly and disobedient girl were filming the incident.

Deputy Fields was fired from his job a few days later. Can you say reward? This girl was rewarded for disobedience. Her cell phone obsession and refusal to obey three different authority figures was rewarded with the officer being fired from his job.

It's been nearly three years and Ben Fields is now suing the sheriff's department and school district for negligence and defamation. Though he was finally cleared of wrong-doing he said this incident changed his life forever.

Undisciplined youth wreak havoc on society, on their peers, their families and themselves. But there is more than a general lack of good old-fashioned discipline creating serious problems for the youth of today.

Encouraging a victim mentality, causing endless confusion about sexual orientation, who to love, what gender to be, where to go to the bathroom, sexual freedom supposedly without the consequences, promoted to kids who aren't equipped emotionally to handle the physical and mental fallout of destructive relationships. Bullying that is taken to a new level via social media. Violent video games as entertainment. The kids of today are dealing with a host of devastating challenges earlier generations didn't have to contend with.

And finally a common thread among all mass shooters seems to be the lack of a father in their lives.

If you're a father not involved in your child's life, get involved and stay involved; and if you know children in your neighborhood who don't have fathers, take some regular time to be a father-figure to them. You might just save a life.

Let's teach the kids to turn on respect for authority and turn off the devices.

We'll all be happier for it.

Chapter 26

Published September 2018

The guy-in-the-garage and I have an arrangement whenever we go anywhere. He drives. I navigate.

This sounds like a simple arrangement, but there are two very challenging aspects we have to deal with every time we get in that truck.

One, he doesn't listen to most of what I say but he responds as if he is listening and I proceed with the false and troubling assumption that he really heard me and meant the answer he gave.

Second, I frequently get my right and left mixed up.

And as I'm listing these challenges, I'm realizing there is one other problem which I grudgingly admit may be my fault. If you notice, when I was listing item number one, there were actually at least three parts to that problem. So really, that was three problems and not one problem. And maybe the fact that I use an excessive amount of words when I'm communicating and I'm not always accurate in what I'm saying could play a very small role in our communication challenges.

Of course these challenges become a bit more serious when we're traveling 70 miles an hour surrounded by other vehicles in an unfamiliar area and a decision has to be made fairly quickly about whether to go straight, turn right or turn left.

Did I say I get my left and right confused? Imagine when I'm under pressure and frustrated what that does to my ability to remember which is which.

But what exactly is the big deal when one small mistake on my part sends him turning into an airport in a strange city driving a one-ton dually, towing the toy hauler? No, we really didn't need to go to the airport and thankfully even though at first glance it looked like it would be nearly impossible to get out of there with that rig, we were able to recover fairly quickly and without mishap. What that does to the stress level inside the cab of our truck though, I'm sure you can imagine. And how exactly do you share further navigation instructions with a person you're not speaking to after an error like that?

You would think with the availability of smart phones that would do away with the navigation challenges. However my research has proven that it just brings a whole new dimension to the opportunities to have heated discussions while getting lost in an unfamiliar town.

Our navigation challenges I'm forced to admit have stayed consistent through the decades even with the ever changing resources for mapping out routes to adventure. We have had fights over my ability (or lack thereof) to interpret the Thomas Brothers map back in the day, the Rand McNally road atlases gave us opportunities for interesting conversations across the United States and even the Mapquest and Yahoo maps printed out and sometimes even brought along with us have caused problems.

And finally the instantly accessible smart phone maps have proven not to be infallible when I'm the one interpreting the message. First because I couldn't figure out how to use it and didn't even try to learn until we were lost in a huge city with major road construction going on right at the freeway interchange we were supposed to be taking.

Once I did know how to use it, I discovered that I preferred to utilize the step-by-step list rather than watching the little arrow chart our progress on the map. However, recently as we were getting off a freeway I didn't understand one of the directions and thinking I knew the area anyway, I told the guy-in-the-garage "turn left up here and then just go straight." Well as we were proceeding straight we passed the street we were supposed to be on. Oh, instant light went off in my head as I said "Oh, that's what that direction meant!" I'm sure he didn't like hearing that comment. It goes without saying he had to make yet another U-turn that day. Some directions just don't make sense until it's 30 seconds too late.

Then there was the time we made multiple, I'm talking multiple U-turns before we found the place we were going to and this time it wasn't even my fault.

Delivering some truck seats to a guy we had both his verbal directions and the smart phone. Yet we could not find the street we were supposed to turn on. It was a fairly small side street off a busy road with lots of fast moving traffic. There was no turn lane so we didn't have much time to watch for the street signs and make the turn. Drove by once and realized a few blocks away we had missed the street. Turned around drove back by, missed the street again. We did this a third time and finally I took the phone map off the step-by-step list and put it on the moving arrow map. Wow. There was the street right ahead, we were bearing down on it according to my little arrow. "Turn here!" I yelled even though there was no visible street sign and the street itself was nearly hidden by trees. Turns out the sign was missing! One small tidbit of info the guy forgot to mention.

And my most recent discovery about our difficulties: It really makes navigational problems even worse when we aren't even on the same page about where exactly we are going.

Recently we were scouting out new stores to put magazine racks in and we had a particular place in mind that was very far from home. We had seen the place the previous month when we were out, but didn't get a chance to stop by. However once we got in the area and were having trouble finding the destination we briefly discussed trying out a travel center we were passing by. But we decided to keep looking for the original place first before we settled on the second choice.

So there we were roaming around in tons of traffic, making U-turns of course, when suddenly I spotted a street that I knew would take us to the original destination.

"So do you want to go to the first place we were looking for?" I asked him and when he said "yes" I very wrongly assumed he was actually listening to what I had said. So I told him "Turn here!"

He was able to make the sudden left turn and I was triumphant as I saw our original destination several blocks ahead. However unbeknowst to me he was looking for the second choice, hadn't seen the place I saw several blocks ahead and before I knew it he burst out "This isn't the right way!" Before I could even answer he hopped on the freeway entrance that we were passing and headed for home. Home that was nearly three hours away.

I silently exploded inside. I wanted to yell: "We were right there! Right! There!" But I'm not a yeller. Instead I quietly made myself a promise I had promised myself thousands of times before. "I will never be his navigator again. I will never go with him when he is going somewhere he has never been before. I absolutely will never do that again! And this time I really mean it!" And I repeated those words inside my head all the way home.

The next morning found him on Craigslist searching for a new desert bike and, at last, there was the exact bike he wanted to buy. In a city three hours away.

"Can you figure out how to get there?" he asked.

Within minutes I had the map printed out.

But don't think I broke my promise to myself that quick.

No, I came up with a genius plan.

I casually suggested that it would probably be a fun trip for him and a friend to take.

Wow, he loved the idea and so did his riding buddy who lived nearby. In fact the friend drove and the guy-in-the-garage got to be the navigator.

A few hours after they left I got a call giving me the good news about the bike being just what he wanted, said they had it loaded and were going to get lunch.

"So did you have any trouble finding the place?" I asked.

A moment of silence. "Just a few wrong turns," he said and then came the great admission: "Being the navigator is kind of challenging."

Ya think?

Chapter 27

Published October 2018

The year was 1982 and the man said we were making a big mistake. But we just went ahead with what we were doing. Twenty-eight years later it finally dawned on us. That man knew what he was talking about and we should have listened to him. "Better late than never," as the saying goes.

But I'm getting ahead of myself. In honor of our 36th anniversary this month, let me start at the very beginning.

It was springtime in 1982 when the guy in the garage made the fantastic discovery on a street corner in Santee CA. A single-seat Funco off road car for sale. He had to have it, he said. We didn't have the money, I told him. He'd sell the Chenowth dune buggy to get it, he said. I pondered that one. I thought the dune buggy was for both of us. How does that work out for me if we sell the two-seat dune buggy to buy a one-seat race car? You get to watch me race it, he said.

Shortly after we got the yellow car he did what he does with every vehicle that comes into his garage or shop. He completely dismantled it, piece by piece and re-built it to his liking.

Now, where to race it? We lived a hop, skip and a jump away from the old South Bay Speedway on Otay Mesa in south San

Diego County. Shortly after we got the car they began holding Sunday afternoon sportsman short course races. You could race all afternoon for only $25. What a deal!

Unfortunately not enough drivers were showing up to make it worthwhile for the promoters to continue the events. There was talk of ending them unless a way could be found to bring in more drivers.

Racing the Funco at South Bay Speedway in 1982. The adventure that led to the start of the magazine 36 years ago!

So we got to thinking. And that is how this magazine got started. Our first thought was a flier to distribute to all the off road shops, but within minutes as the guy-in-the-garage and I were exchanging ideas the flier turned into a newsletter, which some months later turned into a magazine.

Once we made the decision to begin the publication we needed a name and we came up with *San Diego Off Roader*.

That's when we met the man who said we were making a mistake. He had no involvement in the off road industry or sport. But he was a successful businessman. We should have listened to him. His objection was having the name "San Diego" as part of it. You're limiting yourself, he said, it will affect your growth.

We already had the first issue published by the time we met him. We ignored his advice and continued on with the adventure we knew nothing about, save for a few years of high school journalism and a mom who owned the typesetting equipment that enabled us to produce the publication. The newspaper or newsletter, we didn't really know what it was, continued on as a hobby and despite the fact that we thought we had put everything we could possibly think of to print in the first issue, we did manage to continue to come up with information to fill subsequent issues.

The years passed and we realized this hobby was growing into a business that took quite a bit of time. The race track that inspired us eventually shut down altogether, and by now we were calling ourselves a magazine. In 1995 we dropped the "er" and became known as simply *San Diego Off Road*. It had now become my full-time job.

As we moved into the 21st century we were discovering that we had readers from many places outside of San Diego, even outside of California. The events we were covering were also held in places outside San Diego County. Attending off road trade shows and events in other counties to hand out magazines, we discovered that some people would not pick up the magazine because it had "San Diego" in the name. They weren't from San Diego, they said, so there probably wasn't anything of interest to them in there.

That's about the time we added the wording on the cover that said "Serving the counties of Imperial, Los Angeles, Orange, Riverside, San Bernardino, San Diego & Beyond."

That's a lot for someone to read who is just walking past your vendor booth at a busy show. Apparently they never read past "San Diego." Numerous times I would repeat the mantra "We're based in San Diego, we're not just about San Diego."

In 2004 we moved to Ocotillo Wells, so now we were publishing an off road magazine right in the midst of the off road activity. The guy-in-the-garage came on board full-time and we discovered it was quite a kick to be writing about off roading at the same time you could hear vehicles roaring through the desert. Now we were barely in San Diego County ourselves. A couple miles to the east and we'd be out of it.

In the summer of 2009 we followed through on some advice our accountant had given us 10 years earlier. (Yeah, we're a little slow to catch on to some things.) Get incorporated, he had told us. Our corporate name became S&S Publishing, Inc., the S&S for Steve & Sherri. Later that year it finally dawned on us, "Why not follow that other advice we heard in 1982?" Instead of coming up with a geographical description to replace San Diego, we just went with the S&S from our corporate name and that's how we became *S&S Off Road Magazine*.

The name may have changed a few times through the years but we're still the same people.

The guy-in-the-garage is still bossing me around all day every day and still telling anyone who asks that I am the boss.

Some things never stay the same and other things never change!

Chapter 28

Published November 2018

Communicating with the guy-in-the-garage seems to be growing more difficult with each passing year.

But one thing stays consistent throughout the difficulties. Whatever the problem is, it's my fault it happened.

Take for instance last week on trash day. I was really concerned the trash man wasn't coming to empty our dumpster.

We live on a dirt road in a rural area where there is no residential trash service, so we have a commercial account with a small dumpster that gets picked up every other Wednesday.

However recently there was a new driver assigned to the route and he missed our place. Fortunately they sent him back when we called and pointed out the error.

So now I've become like a "trash man lookout." When I go for a walk in the mornings I can hear the truck making stops at other places up and down the road for about a mile away. From my vantage point on the trail I walk on I can see him heading south and I can see him heading north and I know if he has missed turning up our dirt road.

I might add that it was my keen eye a couple months ago that caught him missing our road and my quick thinking that caused us to make a phone call that got the dispatcher to turn him around and come back. So I know the importance of being a "trash man lookout."

This particular morning happened to be the week of Columbus Day. And sure enough it appeared that our very full dumpster was about to not get picked up again.

Unfortunately for both of us the guy-in-the-garage happened to be in the vicinity of the trail I was walking on and I told him that I was pretty sure the trash man was going to miss us again. He seemed completely unconcerned. I felt it was my duty to make sure he shared my obsessive concern. "I'm telling you he's in the area and he missed our road again!" I insisted. He casually said "I told you, he'll probably come tomorrow. He's probably a day late because of the holiday."

I growled, then said "I told you I saw him in the area, he already went south and north and passed our road twice." He repeated somewhat patronizingly "He'll probably come tomorrow." After some more grumbling and insisting on my part that I was right and he was wrong, he continued to ignore me and I finally realized the conversation was over.

I knew we both had more important things to do that day than argue about when the dumpster was going to get emptied so I let the matter drop.

Until the next morning. Out on my walk again, picking up bits and pieces of trash that had been blowing around in the desert, I headed down to our dumpster to drop them in and was dumbfounded because the dumpster was empty. Totally empty. Not a single piece of paper in it. How could that have happened? I never saw the truck come the day before and it for sure hadn't come that morning.

I sought out the guy-in-the-garage, much to my regret, and said "Did you know the trash man came?" I asked in disblief.

"Yeah," he said nonchalantly. "He came yesterday." And I might add that the offhand way he said it, it was as if we had never had an in-depth major conversation about the truck missing our house the day before.

"But when? I was out walking the whole time he was in the area yesterday and I never saw the truck." Believe me you can't miss the sound of that huge blue lumbering trash truck bumping and rumbling up our 1/2 mile dirt road.

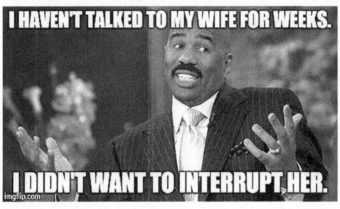

It's not this bad yet in our household, but I could see it easily reaching this level. Might be time for a change.

He patted me on the shoulder in a very condescending way. "Don't you worry about it, didn't I tell you I had it all under control?" he said smirking.

"Wait a minute" I demanded, "You don't even remember telling me yesterday that he was going to come today because of the holiday." He looked at me like I was nuts, then he started laughing and walked away.

So today on my walk, once again it's Wednesday, but I know and the guy-in-the-garage knows it's not "our" Wednesday. I could see and hear the trash truck from afar off and so I purposely sought out the guy-in-the-garage because I wanted to tell him "I hear the trash man and he's not even coming up our road again!" I thought it would be a pretty hilarious way to start the day.

However when I found him he was dealing with a dead battery in a truck he was trying to start and I realized it probably wasn't the best time to make my stupid trash truck joke, so I just kept it to myself.

But turns out I would have an enormous opportunity later in the day to completely annoy him with one of my stories. Sadly I thought I was just giving him some important information he would want to know.

We were making a long drive to check out the magazine rack in one of our desert travel center locations and on the way he happened to ask me "Is that new website company doing what they're supposed to be doing?"

Wow, did I get excited about that question and was more than happy to answer it.

"It's working out really well," I told him enthusiastically. "This company is really doing everything they said they would do. I didn't expect them to be as good as their marketing info said they were."

Then I launched into a detailed explanation of all the background changes they had made to the website in the last three weeks with pretty much play-by-play technical descriptions of not only what they did but how they did it and what kind of impact it should have over time on our website traffic.

I was so excited about the results we're getting from this company that I guess I failed to realize the guy-in-the-garage was experiencing major informational overload from my answer.

When I finally finished answering, he leaned over and looked at me like I had just recited word for word all 26 volumes of the Encyclopedia Brittanica. I think his eyes were almost bulging out.

"Oh," I said. "Should I have just said 'yes they are'?"

He was almost speechless. I say almost because he did manage to let me know I had said way too much.

I still want to burst out laughing everytime I remember the horrified expression on his face.

Oh well, just another day of communicating in paradise. I'm starting to wonder why he doesn't just run the other way when he sees me coming.

Chapter 29

Published December 2018

There are no shortages of double standards around this place we call home and work.

Earlier in the year we visited the topic of the guy-in-the-garage who has no problem expecting me to wait for his needs but he won't wait a single second for something I need. Apparently it's a common trait as we heard from wives and girlfriends around the globe (or maybe just arcross the county!).

Even after writing about that topic, it didn't change things. Recently as I was working on putting together an issue of the magazine the guy-in-the-garage mentioned he needed my help doing a few things on our latest off road vehicle acquisition. It's not actually an off road vehicle, but it's one that keeps us comfortable when we go off roading. We picked up an older model toy hauler some months ago and he was getting it ready for it's maiden voyage.

I, as usual, dropped everything I was doing and drove down to the property where he was working on the vehicle. I was happy to do everything I had volunteered to do, but when I finished up and was ready to head back to my magazine production responsibilities, he said "I'm leaving now too, so can you wait a minute and help me close the ramp door?" I understood the need since it's an older trailer and the springs that are supposed to help close it seem to think it's better to just leave that job to me.

"Sure, I can help with that," I said. And then I waited for him to come out of the trailer so we could close it. But instead he kept painstakingly working at the tedious job of doing some window maintenance. I waited. And I waited some more. I thought about all the work that was waiting on me. I sighed loudly. He looked over and said "I'm almost done."

I sat down in a huff on the ramp door we were supposed to be closing and then I said something way out of character for me. "You just don't get it, do you?!"

"Get what?" he said, barely paying attention because his window detail work was far more fascinating than listening to a wife gripe about waiting.

"I just wrote an article about you making me wait all the time and you're doing it again."

He looked offended. Genuinely. "How does he do that?" I wondered. How does he constantly get away with making me wait on him but if I utter so much as a complaint about it, like he does to me, he looks like I've let him down in the biggest way.

I just want to know how he makes me feel obligated to wait, but he won't wait a nano-second on me. Even after publicly shaming him in print. It's a technique I need to learn.

And so I waited and waited and finally he finished up.

Today was another story, recognizing my busy schedule he never once summoned me to the shop or anywhere else to offer help. I made lots and lots of progress and just about late afternoon, early evening when it's time to begin thinking about what's for dinner, the phone rings.

The caller ID misled me into believing it was a prominent off road shop calling, probably wanting to buy a big expensive full color ad for this issue.

I eagerly picked up the phone only to discover it was a political survey and this guy was good because he had me hooked before I even realized I was already taking the survey.

Well since politics are important to me and stating my opinion equally as important, I decided to go ahead and complete the survey.

Two important things, though, that I did not realize about my decision. One this survey was way too long and two, the guy-in-the-garage chose this exact time to close up his shop, come up to my office and declare he was famished and it was dinner time.

He was patient with my telephone distraction until he discovered what the call was actually about. Then he was, shall we say, not patient?

When I finally got off the phone and headed into the kitchen where he was looking half-starved, he began making snide remarks about me taking a long survey right at dinner time.

"Do you realize, that you might show up here to eat dinner anytime between 4:30 and 7:30 p.m. and expect to eat right then without me ever knowing what time you're going to decide to quit your projects and come up for dinner?"

"That sounds about right," he said with that annoying half smirk/half smile that always seems to get him his way.

Thankfully a really good dinner from the night before had created plenty of leftovers for tonight so we were able to fill our plates fairly quickly.

But he wouldn't let up on this political survey I just took, as if I was a sucker for even getting involved in it.

"Look!" I said forcefully, "I like taking surveys!"

Now he really looked disgusted, but before he could get another word out, I asked him, "Do you know how much time we spend doing things you want to do?"

Without hesitation, he said "Sure, about 99.9% of the time, give or take a percent or two." Then he smiled as he bit into the baked chicken I had prepared for him. "Is that a problem?" he asked nonchalantly while enjoying the chicken.

His answer was so ridiculous I couldn't do much more than laugh.

But fair or not fair, it's how we roll. And after nearly four and a half decades of doing it that way I don't see much chance of that changing. And to tell you the truth, as long as there are smiles and laughter I don't much care which one of us decides what we're doing or how we're spending our time.

But honestly I could do with just a little less waiting. Either that or I need to carry a good book with me to occupy myself in the downtime each time he calls me to help him "for a minute."

Chapter 30

Published February 2019

The white telltale puff of smoke was the first indicator that this big red truck had seen better days.

But old faithful got us to our destination that evening to hang out with the Wednesday night group of kids at church. Five hours later as we pulled up to our gate it gave up the ghost, faithful to the end. Got us all the way home down the dark desert highway, hanging on til the most convenient place of all to be stranded in a broken down vehicle. Home.

It took a few weeks, a lot of phone calls, and some dismantling of the diesel engine to come to a decision. Time to retire big red and find a replacement.

None of us were happy about it. The guy-in-the-garage, the granddaughter-in-the-garage, nor myself. We loved that old truck, except for the fact that it had no heat in the winter and precious little AC in the summer. But that was all fixable. This most recent problem was not the kind of fixable we wanted to get involved with.

And so the hunt for a replacement started. But it's hard when you want almost exactly what you already had.

It's even harder with uncooperative search engines and even more uncooperative sellers.

This should be no problem, I thought, with modern technology. Sat right down and typed in "one ton dually 4wd gas engine stick shift."

A variety of half ton, two wheel drive, automatic diesel powered trucks and a handful of sedans popped up. Not what I'm looking for. At all.

Night after night, for what seemed like weeks the search continued.

Occasionally a promising post appeared. Except for the fact that some of the sellers are more into art than sales and rather than just full on photos of the truck, we'd see some artsy-looking back-to-front driver's side photo, that gave you a real good shot of one taillight as you stared down the side of a truck you could barely see. How about the other side? Could we see the other side? Sure, if you want another awesome photo, this time of the passenger side taillight while you're staring down that side of the truck. Made me wonder if the middle of the tailgate was missing..

How about the photos where you have to tip your head to look at it straight on and you don't know if they were being artsy or just tipping the bottle before they took the photo.

Then the day came when we found one with plenty of great photos and very descriptive text. Surely it seemed this truck was what we were looking for. Only problem is instead of the truck being in the city it was advertised to be in, the seller said it was now located in Mexico and we could follow him across the border and to the town where the truck was being stored. No thank you.

A day or two later another nearly perfect one surfaced. We'd come to the conclusion we were going to have to settle for an automatic transmission rather than the six speed we loved, and even though this one wasn't the dually we wanted, it seemed right in every other way including awesome low mileage.

But when we got there we discovered one small problem. Well make that three small problems. It wasn't smogged. It needed a tire replaced before it could be driven to the smog shop. It needed to be taken off it's non-op registration status before it could be driven. None of which seemed to be happening any time soon. Cross that one off the list.

It amazed me how many people living right here in the magnificently over-regulated state of California where it's required to have a smog certificate when you sell a vehicle were attempting to sell a vehicle without first getting it smogged.

How about the sellers who included plenty of good photos where you could definitely see the entire truck inside and out. But you could also see the trash and clutter inside the vehicle, dirt on the outside, junk in the bed. Okay, people, nothing like advertising that you're just not into taking care of your vehicle and really can't be bothered to even clean it out when you take pictures to sell it. Those trucks never even made it on the list to get crossed off.

The day came when we had an appointment to drive a few hours away to get a truck that would do. It wasn't the dually we wanted, it wasn't the stick shift and it wasn't even the color we wanted. But admittedly with all our other requirements it seemed a bit much to expect it to be the right color too.

We had run the VIN number with Carfax, knew everything checked out good, set the alarm for the early morning wake-up call so we could hit the road and be there by 9 a.m. But at dawn we discovered we both felt the same lack of enthusiasm and crossed that one off the list.

Later that day we got a text from a seller who had a change of heart and had done the necessary work to make her truck smog-legal and had the cert ready to go.

Before the week was out the big red one-ton dually we had completely fogotten about was ours. Worth waiting for, right down to the color.

Now it was time to sell the old one. The guy-in-the-garage cleaned the outside, cleaned the inside, took a lot of good photos and we posted it on several sites, making sure we didn't make any of the mistakes the annoying sellers made.

And what do you know? We discovered there are annoying buyers out there too.

Within a day or two we had numerous inquiries about the truck but the one that takes the cake came through about four days after we posted the ad. Said he was a Cummins diesel mechanic, offered us less than half what we were asking and encouraged us to take him up on his offer "because with the problems your truck has and the age of it no one will want to touch it."

Couldn't hit delete fast enough and before the day was over we sold it for nearly double what the "expert" offered.

The moral of the story? Watch out for those experts and don't be in a hurry to settle for less than what your dream is whether you're buying a truck or just living life.

Good-bye Dodge. Hello Chevy. Dog is wondering where this truck came from.

Chapter 31

Published August 2019

I looked into her empty eyes. Were they really empty or was that fear and confusion I saw? Once again I reassured her that things were okay. And reminded her it was nighttime and everyone was in bed and asleep and that's where she should be too. Well, almost everyone. I was up late again, trying to get some work done during the only uninterrupted period of time I could find.

This is my mom. Only it isn't really my mom. I said good-bye to her quite some time ago. I'm just not sure exactly when that was. And I know I never really uttered the words "good-bye." In fact it only recently hit me that my mom as I knew her, is gone.

Dementia comes on slowly, but one day lets you know for sure it is here and it has to be dealt with. Now. In our case it was the middle of the night phone call when she was lost 50 miles from home driving her truck on the wrong side of the highway. The California Highway Patrol rescued her and placed the call to my sister in Utah, who then called us.

That was not quite two years ago and it's been a roller coaster ride as we learn new ways to cope with the changes life has thrown our way. We have days filled with laughter and days filled with tears, days filled with overwhelming responsibility and sometimes just ordinary days. It's amazing how in the midst of trials, an ordinary day can seem like a huge blessing.

Every year in our August issue we give honor to volunteers. Typically off road volunteers. And for the most part volunteers have sought out a task and chosen to get the job done.

But sometimes we find ourselves volunteering for something that we never quite asked for or imagined might come our way. For instance, caring for an aging parent.

If it hadn't been for my mom, this magazine most likely would not exist.

Me and my mom, 2016

My mom never had much money. Paying the bills each month was a struggle for her, but she always had her dreams.

She worked hard and she dreamed big. When she suddenly found herself a single mom back in the early 1970's, she started a typing service in her home. That was in the days when IBM Selectric typewriters were the latest in technology. She was able to buy one on the installment plan.

Not quite 10 years later she upgraded her typing service to a typesetting service by purchasing what was then state-of-the-art Compugraphic typesetting equipment. I'll never understand how she got the financing to make that happen, because from the first payment on she was behind and there were constant threats that the machine was going to be repossessed. Yet she kept dreaming and kept smiling.

My mom being honored for thousands of hours of helping churches in San Diego County with their Vacation Bible School programs. May 2012

I remember one day when a customer was asking her how business was, she smiled and said "Great!" and I knew that wasn't true at all. When he left, I said, "You'd probably say business was great even if they were here repossessing your equipment while the customer was asking you the question."

"You're probably right!" she smirked.

She never got rich. Not even close. But it was that typesetting equipment that I learned how to operate so I could help her run her business, that ultimately enabled us to start up a little hobby back in 1982, an off road publication that eventually turned into a full-time business for us.

In recent years, she loved driving around in her truck with the large *S&S Off Road Magazine* decals on the sides and handing out magazines to anyone she encountered who she thought might be interested.

As we went through all of her possessions, I saw booklet after booklet, notebooks filled with notes, magazine cut-outs, computer print-outs of dreams, dreams and more dreams.

What kept her going all these years, in addition to her faith in God, were her dreams for the future. It brought tears to my eyes the books from the 1960's she still had with ideas for home-based businesses and ways to make money. She never made it big in a financial way, but the fact that she never lost her ability to dream tells me that maybe making it big isn't just measured monetarily.

Maybe it's measured in our ability to keep going. To walk by faith not by sight. To always be reaching out for a better day even when the day we're living in might not seem so wonderful.

The Bible says in the book of Proverbs "Where there is no vision, the people persish."

I think my mom knew that. And she wasn't about to perish for lack of vision.

A healthy sense of humor has carried her though many hard times and still carries her through today.

In her stage of dementia, she is aware that things aren't quite right. She's aware that we have to take care of her in ways she never imagined and she is aware that her brain isn't working correctly. But she hasn't lost her ability to laugh I discovered when one day recently, she sat on her bed whimpering and asked, "Am I losing my mind?"

"You lost that a long time ago!" I told her and then together we laughed.

It sure beats crying.

Footnote: *A few months after this article was originally published in 2013, Juanita requested to be moved to a care facility. She continued to deteriorate, eventually losing the ability to walk, talk and laugh. However she kept her gentle and pleasant spirit until the summer night in 2019 when the angels escorted her to heaven.*

Chapter 32

Published October 2019

Our greatest natural resource is the minds of our children," Walt Disney believed.

This past week millions of children across the US and around the globe skipped school to take part in Climate Strike Day. Educators condoned this. Adults in their lives condoned this. The media not only condoned it, they promoted it across the news waves for hours on end.

The youth carried signs that read: Fight for Climate Justice, Our House Our Planet, You'll Die of Old Age We'll Die of Climate Change, Only Fossils Like Fossil Fuel. And the saddest. A young man supposing he looks like Jesus carried a sign that said "I Don't Want To Die For Your Sins Again."

Their leader? Greta Thunberg, a 16-year-old Swedish girl. She took the world by storm a year ago when she did a one-man Climate Strike outside of her school. And just like that she's a media sensation. She's worshipped and followed by millions. She sailed on a solar-powered boat across the ocean to preach to the United States Congress. We need to "shame those who need shaming" is her mantra as she lays blame at the feet of the United States Congress and anyone else who dares to use fossil fuel. She claims we're facing the imminent destruction of the world. And millions of young people jumped on the band wagon. The photos are disheartening. Young people around the world buying into the cult of environmentalism. And parents and teachers encouraging them.

Do we blame the kids? It's tempting, especially considering what Australian broadcaster, Alan Jones, said:

"To all the school kids going on strike for climate change, you're the first generation who have required air conditioning in every room. You want TV in every room, and your classes are all computerized. You spend all day and night on electronic devices.

"More than ever, you don't walk or ride bikes to school, but you arrive in caravans of private cars that choke suburban roads and worsen rush hour traffic.

"You're the biggest consumer of manufactured goods ever and update perfectly good expensive luxury items to stay trendy. Your entertainment comes from electric devices.

"How about this? Tell your teacher to turn off the air-con, walk or ride to school, switch off your devices and read a book, make a sandwich instead of buying manufactured fast food.

"But none of this will happen because, you're selfish, badly educated, virtue-signaling little turds inspired by the adults around you who crave a feeling of having a noble cause while they indulge themselves in western luxury and unprecedented quality of life. Wake up, grow up, and shut up until you're sure of the facts before protesting." [1]

I'm very inclined to put the blame on the adults, the ones guilty of misleading the young people and using them to promote their agenda.

John Nolte writes on Breitbart.com: "For more than 50 years Climate Alarmists in the scientific community and environmental movement have not gotten even one prediction correct, but they do have a perfect record of getting 41 predictions wrong."[2]

What is the ultimate motivation to push an agenda that is so consistently wrong? The almighty dollar.

It's no mere coincidence that the day Greta Thunberg was a one-man Climate Strike team a zealous eco-profiteer by the name of Ingmar Rentzhog just "happened" to be walking by. He witnessed the protest, took photos and launched a viral social media frenzy.

The Global Warming Policy Forum reported on August 19, 2019: "The Greta phenomenon has also involved green lobbyists, PR hustlers, eco-academics and a think tank founded by a wealthy former minister in Sweden's Social Democratic government with links to the country's energy companies. These companies are preparing for the biggest bonanza of government contracts in history: the greening of the western economies. Greta, whether she and her parents know it or not, is the face of their political strategy."[3]

There are too many untrustworthy adults in education, in politics, in movies, in social media, leading our children down a path that fills them with worry, fear, anxiety and to borrow from an old song "looking for love in all the wrong places." A recent headline in the L.A. Times reads: "Suicide rates for U.S. teens and young adults are the highest on record."[4]

Verbal pollution is a greater threat to the kids than climate change. The F word is everywhere, in headlines, text messages, on T-shirts, in songs and flowing frequently out of the mouths of adults and kids in almost every setting. Kids are not immune to reading it and hearing it on an almost daily basis.

They're told they can choose what sex they want to be and no one can tell them any different. Kids who can't decide what they want at the candy store are encouraged to believe they were not born with a God-given sex assignment, but it's up to them to decide. And alphabet activists embrace the opportunity to promote their lifestyle by pushing the kids front and center whether it's at pride parades, drag queen story hours or encouraging gender confusion. It makes the news and promotes the cause. But at what expense?

Micro computers in the form of smart phones are handed out to kids with unnerving frequency, when you realize the magnificent capability to access evil that is in those devices. Millions of kids are carrying them around in their pockets with the opportunity to view and post anything on the web with very little supervision. Cyberbullying, social media obsession and game addiction, all available instantly at their fingertips. Tech savvy kids can hide their activities so that even parents who are checking on them, may not catch all that is going on.

All this combined with the billion dollar green industry now jumping on the bandwagon of brainwashing kids to broadcast their marketing message to the world is just another indicator of the sad lack of regard for the minds of children.

Am I concerned about climate change? No. Do I think there is a natural resource in serious danger of destruction? You bet I do. And in the words of Walt Disney, it's "our greatest natural resource."

The minds of our children.

[1] https://www.redstate.com/brandon_morse/2019/09/21/watch-australian-broadcaster-takes-spoiled-climate-protesting-students-epic-fashion/
[2] https://www.breitbart.com/environment/2019/09/20/nolte-climate-experts-are-0-41-with-their-doomsday-predictions/
[3] https://www.thegwpf.com/greta-thunberg-and-the-plot-to-forge-a-climate-warrior/
[4] https://www.latimes.com/science/la-sci-suicide-rates-rising-teens-young-adults-20190618-story.html

Chapter 33

Published November 2019

I did something recently I've been wanting to do since I was a kid.

I wrote a book. A mystery for kids. I grew up reading mysteries. Loved them. I also loved writing and wrote my first story in fifth grade.

Didn't know at the time that the guy-in-the-garage and I were going to school together when I wrote that story. He didn't know that either. A few years later when we met as teenagers and discovered we both went to the same elementary school, he told me that he and his friends used to throw dodge balls at the girls and hit them in the face. He was 18 and still seemed to think that was pretty funny.

"So that was you?" my 16-year-old self said, staring right into his eyes, not smiling.

He laughed even harder when I told him I got hit in the nose with a dodge ball when I was in fifth grade.

Apparently the dodge ball slamming into my face didn't cause any brain damage because I went on to write stories into my early 20's. Eventually I got some of them published, but my real goal was to write a book. I used to imagine I would be the youngest person ever to get a book published. But as the years went by my procrastination caused me to miss that goal. So then I decided to just bide my time and be the oldest person ever to have a book published. Obviously I wasn't super motivated.

It was more than procrastination though. Life happened. Publishing the magazine, raising a family, starting an off road camp, caring for elderly parents. Before I knew it 40 some years had passed. But I never forgot I wanted to write a book someday.

This past New Year's eve I set a goal to write my book before 2019 came to an end. I already knew the title and the gist of the story. It had been floating around in my head for nearly 15 years, almost since we moved to the desert. I made a list of things I needed to change in my schedule so that I would have time to write and for the first five months of the year nearly every night starting around 9 p.m. I worked on the book, sometimes until midnight.

I'm beyond excited (and you can verify that with the guy-in-the-garage) to say that book one of MotoMysteries was published in October and is available on Amazon and a variety of other places.

The Skeleton and the Lantern, Book 1 of MotoMysteries, is available on Amazon. Visit www.sherrikukla.com for more info on MotoMysteries

But there is another part to this story that I feel compelled to share.

When I get excited about something I tend to talk about it. A lot. Like from the moment I wake up until either I go to bed, or everyone else in the house goes to bed, and no one is around to listen to me. If that happens then I just text my night owl aunt in

Kansas, who patiently responds to every single one of my texts talking about the book. Every. Single. One. And I'm telling you that is a lot.

The guy-in-the-garage has pointed out to me once or twice that I'm talking about the book quite a bit. An excessive amount. I agreed and I told him, I totally understand what it's like to have to listen to me go on and on. Because I've been listening to him talk about motorcycles for 45+ years.

"I'm going to the shop to work on the motorcycles," he will say. Then when he gets there he will call me. "Can you get on eBay and order those parts I have on the watch list?" or "Can you get on Partzilla and look up the diagram for this 1967 Kawasaki?" or "Can you search google and figure out why I'm not getting spark on this hybrid Banshee motorcycle I'm building?"

Or how about this? Gets off the phone from talking to a guy in Texas about a motorcycle he wants and says to me "I think we'll go to Texas and get this bike."

"Okay, when?" I ask.

"Tonight," he says.

Recently we had company over (with their motorcycles of course) and I went to the hall closet to find sheets for the beds in the trailer and there were none. Something tells me I will find every single sheet I'm missing covering up all the vintage motorcycle restorations he's done for the past 10 years.

And how about when we go racing in the dead of winter and it's freezing out. Do you think the people get first pick of the available blankets in the fifth wheel? No, first all the race bikes get covered with blankets and then we choose what's left.

So when it comes to getting a little obssessed about the things we're excited about, it's safe to say we're pretty much just the same.

And one final point that comes to mind about this new adventure we're on with the book.

When I first came up with the idea for MotoMysteries many years ago, I wrote a couple of chapters and submitted them to an online critique group. The response I got from the one lady who read it was not very positive. She pretty much marked up every line of every page and suggested I read some books on editing and didn't really have anything positive to say. So I put it away. For almost 15 years.

But the idea would not go out of my head. The first day of January, I pulled those chapters out, and printed them for the granddaughter to read

She loved the story, and had some really good positive suggestions. I wrote another 40 or 50 pages and she kept reading as I completed each chapter. But then I got discouraged and decided I wasn't going to follow through with this project after all.

She would not let me quit. And it was her encouragement that caused me to persevere and see the project through to the end.

The words we speak to those around us can make all the difference in the world in the outcome of a situation, or even a life.

Speak words of encouragement. You might change the world just with your words.

Chapter 34

Published December 2019

I met the guy-in-the-garage during the spring of my 16th year. By Christmas I knew the way to this guy's heart was not through his stomach.

He was 18 and had to rely on using his dad's tools to do what he's been doing since I met him in 1973. Working on motorcycles. Taking them apart. Putting them back together.

After the honeymoon period of our early dating days, we mostly hung out at my house watching TV in the evenings. Old re-runs of Perry Mason would be on the set and he'd sit on the couch with the Sears catalog in his lap opened to the tool section. That catalog was dog-eared on every Craftsman page by the time Christmas rolled around.

I knew very quickly what it would take to win this guy's heart forever more.

I mostly pretended to be trying to figure out who the killer was on that night's episode but out of the corner of my eye I was closely watching which tool set he was the most interested in.

I made $1.75 an hour and knew I'd have to devote more than one paycheck to buy him the tools he was longing for.

When the time came to place my order I settled on the 45-piece set that included a tool box. The $50 price tag was about all I could afford, although there were plenty other larger kits I would have preferred. I remember the disappointment when I went to the catalog department turns to pick up my order and discovered the tool box it said it came with was plastic not metal.

However that plastic tool box, complete with tools inside, including a reversible ratchet, was definitely a hit and by the following Christmas we were married.

Not sure what I gave him that year since now instead of just using our paychecks to have fun, we had to stretch our wages to cover electricity, food, gas and rent. We skipped a phone and insurance. We had to have some money to play around with.

Our Biggest
CRAFTSMAN
REG. U.S. PAT. OFF.
Tool Set
195 pieces
in all

Includes
¼, ⅜, ½ and
¾-inch
drive parts

Only
$**189**⁹⁵
Without cabinet

From the 1973 Sears catalog. I really would have preferred getting this tool set for him way back in our early days, but at $1.75 an hour that just wasn't going to happen. As it turns out the 45-piece set did the job quite nicely.

In the years to come we grew more confident in our ability to provide for ourselves, and Christmas gifts included a welding helmet, state-of-the-art (for the 1970's) motorcycle stand complete with work bench, and eventually even a dune buggy. At $400, that one Christmas, I thought we were just about breaking the bank. But that purchase provided months of fun for both of us.

I'd like to say it provided years of fun, but it wasn't long before he was on to bigger, better, faster in the buggy department. Even though it wasn't even Christmas, he plunked down the money for a new frame and set out to build us a brand new buggy, made to order to his specifications.

We soon discovered some other ways to celebrate Christmas and take extra joy in giving when for several years we adopted a family through the Salvation Army. Some of our readers from the 1980s may remember taking part in that gift giving adventure along with us.

Later, as our family grew, Christmas was all the more fun as we shopped for the kids. Bicycles and G.I. Joes, riding gear, books, puzzles, movies and more.

The kids always knew what to get Dad for Christmas. Tools, tools and more tools.

And so the collection continued to grow far exceeding the original 45-piece tool set, most of which he still has and the projects fairly flew in and out of the garage. Once he started restoring motorcycles a decade or two ago, for himself and others, a whole new way of shopping for parts had become available. The internet. Some days it feels like Christmas all year long as delivery men from far and wide bring parts for the projects. In fact, that's how I let him know a new shipment has arrived. "It's Christmas!" I tell him no matter what month of the year it is.

You've heard it said "Happy wife, happy life," but I find that I actually operate on the reverse theory.

If the guy-in-the-garage (and others around me) have a happy life, then, yes, Virginia, there is a happy wife.

Will you help promote
Parking Precious

Online reviews play a big role in the success of a book. Many readers choose what book to order based on what reviewers have to say. If you could take a few minutes and give an honest review at Amazon.com we would be very grateful.

Thank you for coming along on the adventures with me and the guy-in-the-garage. I hope you're willing to take a few minutes to post a review!

Sherri

Sherri Kukla
S&S Publishing, Inc.
ssormag@gmail.com

P.S. If you'd like, send me an email after you leave a review! We'd love to hear from you and to go on-line and read the review!

ABOUT S&S PUBLISHING, INC.
Sherri Kukla and her husband Steve are the publishers of *S&S Off Road Magazine* and the *MotoMysteries* fiction series for kids ages 9 and up. They reside in the off road community of Ocotillo Wells CA with their teenage granddaughter and a dozen or so motorcycles. Their publishing adventures started in 1982 with the launching of *San Diego Off Roader*, later named *San Diego Off Road Magazine*. In 2008 they incorporated as S&S Publishing, Inc. and changed the name of the magazine to *S&S Off Road* shortly thereafter. Visit their websites at www.ssorm.com and www.sherrikukla.com

Other books by S&S Publishing Inc.
MotoMysteries
Middle Grade Novels that even adults enjoy!

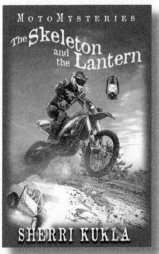

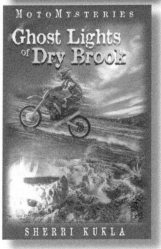

Book 1 – *The Skeleton and the Lantern*
Book 2 - *Ghost Lights of Dry Brook*
Book 3 - *Phantom Ship in the Desert*
Book 4 - *Harbor Point Haunt (due Fall 2021)*

The Christmas Miracle A Christmas Mini-Mystery

www.sherrikukla.com

Magazine Books by S&S Publishing Inc

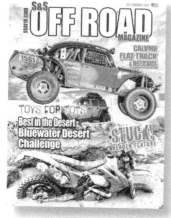
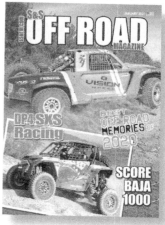

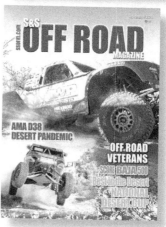

Available on Amazon
Search **S&S Off Road Magazine**

Subscribe to the free Super-Digital edition of
S&S Off Road Magazine
email ssormag@gmail.com and get on the list

Also by S&S Publishing Inc

Available on Amazon
Steve Kukla a.k.a. "the guy-in-the-garage" is a co-author
of this book that is comprised of articles previously published in
S&S Off Road Magazine

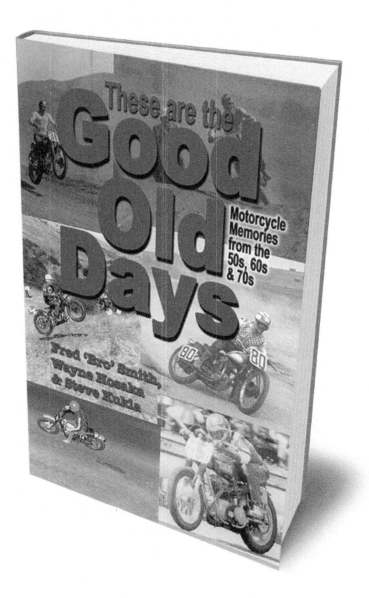